John McCosh

Nuova Italia

Tours and Retours through France, Switzerland, Italy and Sicily

John McCosh

Nuova Italia
Tours and Retours through France, Switzerland, Italy and Sicily

ISBN/EAN: 9783744745727

Printed in Europe, USA, Canada, Australia, Japan

Cover: Foto ©Thomas Meinert / pixelio.de

More available books at **www.hansebooks.com**

OR

TOURS AND RETOURS

THROUGH

FRANCE, SWITZERLAND, ITALY, AND SICILY:

𝔄 𝔓𝔬𝔢𝔪 𝔦𝔫 𝔗𝔢𝔫 ℭ𝔞𝔫𝔱𝔬𝔰.

BY NOMENTINO, F.R.G.S.

Mari terraque, lacu, flumine cœloque, quærens.

LONDON:

LONGMANS, GREEN, AND CO.

1872.

PREFACE.

THE AUTHOR of the following pages has had the privilege of spending many seasons in the classic lands of Italy, and watching her struggles to shake off the constricting coils of superstition and oppression that threatened to strangle her. He lately left her standing statue-like, triumphant, amidst the ruins of empires, principalities and powers, temporal, spiritual, and eternal—A New Italy—A Nuova Italia.

The verses were written almost entirely upon the scenes described, and under the influence of passing events. Their composition added to the enjoyment of many a leisure hour abroad, and the author hopes that their perusal will add to the enjoyment of many a leisure hour at home.

Reserving to himself the Royal Right of Incognito, he now presents them to an Indulgent Public, and launches his Paper Skiff upon the stream of time, to sink or swim, according to its deserts, with the Paternal Benediction,

VA SANO ! VA PIANO ! VA LONTANO !

London: August 1872

CONTENTS.

---◆---

CANTO FIRST.

CANTO SECOND.

a

CANTO THIRD.

CANTO FOURTH.

CANTO FIFTH.

CANTO SIXTH.

CANTO SEVENTH.

CANTO EIGHTH.

CANTO NINTH.

CANTO TENTH.

NUOVA ITALIA

CANTO FIRST

I

WHILST men of wealth and weight are tied to town,
   Oppressed with heat and dust beyond endurance,
In Rotten Row patrolling up and down,
   Or vexing Parliament with smart assurance,
Let us our leathern light portmanteau fill,
And off our landlord ask our little bill.

II

If no broad acres nor big mansions wait
   Our annual autumn visit in suspense,
We've in the mind's eye got a rich estate,
   Fit to content each man of common sense :
All Switzerland is ours for the next quarter,
And who for British scenes its wealth would barter?

III

Italia, too, is ours, far in the distance,
   With all its attributes of art and clime ;
Nova Italia ! with its new existence ;
   United Italy ! once more sublime.
Regenerate Italy asserts her claim,
To stand once more within the dome of fame.

Let us break ground, and at the Crystal Palace
   Complete our pack, and halt there for a day,
And drink to London town a parting chalice,
   And from the heights its world below survey.
Shrouded in smoke, with atmosphere of lead,
Wherein St. Paul's can hardly show its head.

London is grown so mighty in its line,
   Its chimney-smoke is never cleared away !
The noontide sun is rarely seen to shine !
   Even on the best of a midsummer's day !
In winter all's impenetrable gloom,
And gaslight all day through is oft its doom !

How long, ye Legislators, will ye wrangle
   About a Tweedledum and Tweedledee ?
And dare new bills Utopian to mangle,
   Or pass them only in a half degree ?
Subordinating public weal to spite,
And wasting millions to preserve a mite !

You've legislated for the most provoking
   Of public nuisances, the factory stacks ;
But left some million private chimneys smoking,
   To charge the air with smoke and sooty blacks !
There *is* a way this evil to escape.
Go find it out, and a new Smoke Act shape !

VIII

That's the Victoria Tower ! just barely seen
    Above the house where rages party strife ;
Where gladiators fight with rapiers keen,
    With pike, and javelin, and bowie knife.
Where members, proud of their patrician spurs,
Can bark and worry like a pack of curs.

IX

The Cato's now afloat ; the steam is up ;
    The passengers and luggage all aboard ;
And hastily is drained eacn stirrup cup
    'Twixt cit and citizen, 'twixt knight and lord.
The Folkestone piers are past ; a rolling sea
Makes the good boat lurch heavily a-lee.

X

All those who can, secure a vacant berth,
    And those who can't, a seat or plank on deck,
Little disposed for gossip or for mirth,
    Each with an empty basin at his beck ;
Unutterable anguish each one looking,
Sighing and sobbing, retching and even puking.

XI

How long, you two Invincibles, how long,
    You France and England, will you stand the Channel?
And mew and puke, the weak as well as strong,
    Upon its billows, sheathed in furs and flannel,
Turning your insides out, with sighs and groans,
In sad affright at breaking thy old bones ?

XII

When Science tells you, after careful scan,
   From shore to shore a tunnel can be mined,
And engineers stand ready with their plan
   Whenever you Wiseacres are inclined ;
Go ! have a railway underneath the sea,
And from sea-sickness be for ever free !

XIII

The millions you two spent in the Crimea
   Would finish the big job and all its plant,
And realise, in fact, the beau idea ;
   And half seas over both might have a rant
Some five years hence, and to the world declare
The passage free 'tween France and Angleterre.

XIV

Though but two hours were passed upon the sea,
   It seemed a voyage of a week or more ;
And when Boulogne they entered in high glee
   The passengers rushed eagerly ashore,   ·
Regardless of the *gens-d'armes* on the landing,
And female porters with their barrows standing.

XV

How wond:ous was the change in human nature,
   In man and woman, infancy and age !
So queer their dress ; so very low their stature ;
   So odd their every action, even their rage ;
So strange their dogs, carts, horses, donkeys, mules,
Their very wise men, and their very fools.

XVI

Formal and civil were they in *douane*;
    Short was the transit to the railway station,
Our seats secured, our luggage in the van,
    We forward rattled in express rotation,
And reached *Belle Paris* to an evening dinner,
The sea-sick patients looking somewhat thinner.

XVII

Let's take a stroll along the Boulevard—
    The evening's fine, the sun will soon be down—
And mark the changes with all due regard
    Since first we saw the antiquated town,
When smoking lamps were hung across each street,
And flambeaux were in use by the discreet.

XVIII

Old Paris now has almost disappeared !
    New boulevards extend in each direction ;
Whole streets of stone-built palaces are reared,
    New theatres and churches in each section,
Asphaltic pavements skirt each well-swept street,
And stately trees along their margins meet.

XIX

This is no holiday, though you may think so,
    From all those idle loungers and good cheer ;
'Tis but their evening habitude to drink so—
    A cup of coffee or a glass of beer—
To smoke a mild cigar, or even a pipe,
To eat an ice, or suck an orange ripe.

XX

No people happier in the world than they,
  With more prosperity in each man's eyes,
Well fed and clad, well lodged, they no doubt may
  Imagine Paris quite a paradise,
And pity northern strangers when they come
To take a fortnight's holiday from home.

XXI

Nothing in ancient Athens or in Rome
  Could have excelled the edifices here,
Each classic tower, each temple, and each dome
  Has got its counterpart all sharp and clear.
For rustic Rome Augustus did no more
Than did great N. his Paris to restore.

XXII

Now for Geneva and the sky-blue Rhone;
  By train express we've ticketed our places;
Our purses not a little lighter grown
  By heavy bills, made out with best of graces;
But Paris charges for its *beau idéal*
In golden Naps. substantially real.

XXIII

Now 'cross the Seine, that model city river,
  We dash along, o'er bridges and o'er highways,
'Midst gay parterres and aspens at the quiver,
  By sylvan cots and humble hamlets' byways,
The country all as tame, as smooth, and flat,
As is the top of a new Lincoln's hat.

XXIV

The crops in patches ! patrimonial roods !
  From son to son descending in succession ;
Like tools of husbandry, or household goods,
  From ancestors remote in retrogression ;
Each petty ridge with landmarks, wood and stone,
To tell posterity when they are gone.

XXV

Now on through Burgundy our panting steed
  Drags us along in most impetuous course :
We scarce can keep our cushions, and have need,
  For greater safety, to hold on with force,
Halting but seldom in the headlong haste,
Unless to fill up water run to waste.

XXVI

Now gentle hills and dales of rare fertility
  Vary the landscape, pleasing to the view ;
With here and there a bit of bare sterility,
  A cairn of stones, or quarry old or new ;
Whilst vines in hedgerows part the plots of corn,
Or in square leagues the country side adorn.

XXVII

Unlike Italian vines, from tree to tree
  Flaunting their tendrils in profuse disorder,
Each vine is wedded to a stake, you see,
  Not higher than a man, upon the border ;
Claiming the widow's privilege, when rotten
To wed a new one, the old mate forgotten !

XXVIII

The husbandmen in hamlets far apart,
    Far from their vineyards trustingly reposing,
Their houses built in careless rustic art,
    The inmates all, both old and young, disclosing;
Each front festooned with heads of last year's maize,
Proving their easy state of means and ways.

XXIX

Now Beaune and Macon passed (famed for their wine)
    We cross the slowly creeping muddy Soane
Upon a girder bridge, no doubt as fine
    As any to be found 'tween Rhine and Rhone;
And cross its spacious valley, quite amazing !
With herds of sheep and kine, all busy grazing.

XXX

And now the hills expand to lofty mountains,
    Dappled with forests, fruit trees in the glades,
Pouring down water from their woodland fountains
    O'er rock and precipice in white cascades;
Whilst numerous chalets deck their grassy slopes,
And wreaths of snow bestud their naked tops.

XXXI

A masterpiece of modern engineering !
    The railway 's made with most consummate skill,
The train o'er valleys, and through rocks careering,
    Up hill and down hill, at the driver's will,
Through vineyards and through hamlets at the roar,
Where even a dog-cart never ran before.

XXXII

Where goats below pick up their frugal meal,
  And wilder ones above their lives maintain ;
And there stands one, just resting on his heel,
  Eyeing with confidence the rattling train,
Whilst a fond mother and a brace of kids
Browse unconcerned, and hardly lift their lids.

XXXIII

And there the rapid Rhone in ultra-blue,
  Just like a snake gigantic, far below,
Steals through the rocks, magnificent to view !
  Now smooth as oil, now foaming in its flow.
Making one wonder how it found its way
Through all these Jura mountains grim and gray.

XXXIV

'Geneva !' cries the guard.   The crowds descend,
  And fill the platform, though both long and broad.
A dozen omnibuses ready, lend
  A helping hand, all standing on the road.
And soon the multitude to some hotel
Conduct in safety, at one single spell.

XXXV

Geneva, finest city in Swiss land,
  How art thou altered in a score of years !
New bridges, quays, and palaces so grand,
  Portend for thy prosperity no fears,
In every copse a villa neat is shrouded,
And thy sea-lake with sail and steam is crowded.

XXXVI

Here Northern invalids of Teuton race
    A genial winter on its margin find,
With many a sheltered, sunny resting-place ;
    And scenery exactly to their mind ;
With markets filled with stores of every sort,
That make Geneva quite a grand resort.

XXXVII

Here Gibbon, Davy, Rousseau, and Voltaire,
    Dumas and Byron, Goethe and Peel,
Have sought and found asylum from their care ;
    Here Calvin Popery first made to reel,
Preaching against each dogma in rotation,
And sowed the seeds of the great Reformation.

XXXVIII

What panoply of war !   What haste to battle
    In peaceable Geneva, so sedate !
Its town is like a camp, and canons rattle,
    Field guns and heavy guns, at practice rate ;
Musty and rustily they creak along,
Much to the wonder of the passing throng.

XXXIX

Rough are their horses, from their pastures rich,
    Half-shod, half-groomed, ill harnessed, and ill bred ;
Their riders rough, and rustic every stitch,
    Glad of a chance to have their leaders led.
War's very raw material is there,
Wanting in nothing but the serjeant's care.

XL

From all the shop-doors, all the burghers' houses,
    In heavy marching order, *cap-à-pie*,
Smart riflemen are rushing from their spouses,
    Their knapsacks victualled to a high degree,
Followed by their big boys, or buxom wenches,
Bearing warm counterpanes for the cold trenches.

XLI

Their restless neighbours sound the trump of war;
    All France is rampant, rushing to the Rhine ;
And Switzerland, though looking from afar,
    Must man each fortress all along her line ;
Prepared with shot and shell, with lead and pewter,
To fight, or to remain a simple neuter.

XLII

Let's take our passage in the Bonnivard,
    One of a fleet of steamers on Lake Leman ;
As fine a craft as any yachting bard
    Could wish to steam in, though he were a seaman ;
A yacht quite fit to breast the broad Atlantic,
And make all canvas yachtsmen wild and frantic.

XLIII

A crowd of passengers we've got on board,
    Both Swiss and foreigners, of every station :
A brace of English barristers, a lord,
    Some Oxford students fresh for the vacation,
A rev'rend padre poring o'er his book,
A mob of tourists under Captain Cook.

XLIV

A squad of German students, too, is there ;
  A boarding-school of girls in their teens,
Slick from America, as does appear ;
  And Jonathan and Co., proud of their means,
With trunks almost as bulky as a log-house,—
Quite large enough for a Newfoundland dog-house.

XLV

The morning's fresh and fair.   The lazy clouds
  Along the mountain slopes are slumbering still,
Or resting on the Jura.   Idle crowds !
  Watching the sunshine speck each vine-clad hill,
Whilst, robed in mist and sunk in deep repose,
Mont Blanc can barely show his rosy nose.

XLVI

The swans have left their nests on Rousseau's Isle,
  And gone to fish and grub in earnest mood.
The diligence for Chamounix meanwhile
  Cracks off at speed, its list of tourists good.
The city bells strike up their matin chimes,
And thrifty shopmen ope their doors betimes.

XLVII

Now on to Nyon, Thonon, and Lausanne,
  Vevay and Clarence, Montreux and Veytaux,
Ten knots an hour our gallant steamer ran,
  Laughing to scorn the sailing craft so slow ;
For though a railway through each village runs
The lover of the picturesque it shuns.

XLVIII

Here Switzerland at last is realised,
  With all its mountain majesty sublime,
With vineyards rich in wine, so highly prized,
  And a most temperate healthy winter clime ;
Its *Dent du Midi*, dappled o'er with snow,
Reflected in Lake Leman far below.

XLIX

Behold the Rhone ! with overwhelming force,
  Roaring and raging in its mad career ;
Through rocks and meadows tearing its rude course,
  Robbing each village of some roods a year ;
Charging its tawny torrent with the soil
Of injured husbandmen,—those sons of toil !

L

Within man's memory, square miles of silt,
  Now fertile fields, you've dropped into the lake ;
Threatening some future cycle when thou wilt
  So silt it up, and a broad meadow make ;
Drawing upon the Alps for solid matter,
Daring their Schiedecks and their horns to shatter,

LI

Humbling their haughty pride of lofty birth !
  By stern disintegration, year by year,
Lowering their heads unto the very earth,
  Without a qualm of penitence or fear,
By never-ending, strenuous persistence,
Until the Alpine chain has no existence !

LII

What miserable beings have we here ?
  Diseased alike in body and in mind !
Fit only for the grave ! and yet they rear
  A progeny still lower of their kind !
Cumbering the soil with useless population,
And burdening the income of the nation.

LIII

Strange and mysterious are the laws of nature
  That dooms to misery these wretched creatures !
Tainting their blood and stunting them in stature,
  And leaving them with scarcely human features !
Yet Science can't explain the reason why,
At least, the secret does not meet the eye.

LIV

Some say 'tis drinking water charged with lime ;
  Some say 'tis drinking melted snow and ice ;
Some blame the heat and moisture of their clime ;
  Some blame their predilection unto vice.
With better reason, some the cause declare
Is scanty sunshine and most stagnant air,—

LV

Is over-early training unto toil,—
  Especially of women, even when mothers !
No rest for womankind on this hard soil ;
  They toil and drudge just like their busy brothers.
The females of all creatures upon earth
Require protection, from their very birth !

LVI

What have we here? a charnel-house of bones!
  Bare human skulls, exposed with gaunt grimaces,
Heaped one on other like a cairn of stones,
  With smaller bones to keep them in their places.
Still known by name, though, crumbling to decay,
Their wisdom, wit, and beauty passed away!

LVII

Sad sorry relics of the hamlet's pride!
  Mere mockeries of mankind, out of place!
Both friends and foes thus grinning side by side!
  The living and the dead brought face to face!
Some morbid mania, contrived to feed
A bigot's dogma, or a sexton's greed!

LVIII

Let's halt a day at Brieg, that fine old town
  That better days has seen and higher station;
Its palaces all gaunt and tumbled down,
  A world too large for its scant population;
Where roaring torrents stun the dullest ear,
And keep its denizens in constant fear.

LIX

Behold the great Napoleonic way!
  That model masterpiece of engineering,
Fit for the heaviest gun, or largest dray;
  Triumphant, o'er the Simplon pass careering;
Proof against landslips, storms, and avalanches,
Or falling pine trees with their roots and branches.

LX

That's Mont Leone glancing on the top,
　Apparently but two short leagues away ;
But four long hours, without a single stop,
　Will barely take you there, by night or day ;
So very serpentine the road is made,
You'd think that by the *mile*, the job was paid !

LXI

Now up the Eggischorne so steep we climb,
　O'er rock and precipice, upstairs and down,
With giddy head, and footsteps out of time,
　And squat down by the cross upon the crown,
Oppressed with perspiration and with heat,
And panting breath, and pulse at fever-beat.

LXII

When reassured that we could stand upright,
　Without the risk of falling off the summit,
And of the glacier *See* almost in fright,
　Into which anyone could drop a plummet,
We oped our eyes, and saw a scene sublime,
Fit to remember for our course of time !

LXIII

There sat assembled in grave convocation
　The mightiest monarchs of the snowy Alps !
Proud of their pedigree and lofty station,
　Raising to heaven their venerable scalps,
Their shoulders robed in everlasting snow,
Their snowy beards perpetual in their flow !

LXIV

From each broad chest hard glacier streams descended,
   Like streams of water down their gnarled sides,
With others joining as their length extended,
   Till all in one grand glacier merged their tides,
Which like a mighty river down the vale,
Crept imperceptibly.   To which, All hail!

XV

Hail to thee infant Rhone! and to thy cradle!
   Full many a league we've travelled up thy course,
Zu fuss, by vetturino, and by saddle;
   And now we stand beside thy very source,
Within the fountainhead that gives thee birth,
Watching thy first convulsive throes on earth!

LXVI

And that's thy Galenstock against the sky,
   Wrapt in a mantle of perpetual snow,
The Genius of the glacier! from on high ·
   Watching its offspring in its glacial flow;
Tending its infant with fresh freezing water,
With melting snow or solid icy matter.

LXVII

Fit parent for such bounding, boundless river,
   This icy mountain chain of crystal clear;
Melting and freezing daily, nightly, ever,
   In perpetuity from year to year.
Yet ever on the move with downward pace,
Through scarce six inches is its daily race.

LXVIII

Let us ascend the glacier from a shoulder
　That juts upon a spur of solid drift;
The earth is freshly turned upon the boulder,
　As by a ploughshare of prodigious rift,
But though for hours you on the furrow stare.
No other sign of motion find you there !

LXIX

The day is warm, the ice in melting mood ;
　The ice all undulated like a sea ;
Roughened by gravel, and the footing good,
　Studded with stones of great and small degree,
With deep crevasses every here and there,
That open-mouthed cry out the word, BEWARE !

LXX

Brisk little rivers run in every glade,
　Clear as a dewdrop, or Pierian rill,
With lake and pool, and rapid and cascade,
　And power enough to turn a fairy mill,
Here diving out of sight down icy funnels,
There reappearing, from some icy tunnels.

LXXI

But ere the setting of the summer sun,
　Each ice-fed rivulet more feebly flows ;
At dusk its race unto the plains is run,
　And midnight seals all up in still repose ;
And when next day dawns—like a funeral pall
Hoar frost is seen incrusted over all.

LXXII

Just lift that stone embedded in the ice,
  And living creatures you will there survey ;
The guide will tell you, they are glacier lice,
  That dread the light and heat of open day ;
And though they're lithe and active, every joint,
Their temperature must be the freezing point !

LXXIII

Two weary hours we've tramped up icy slopes,
  But now our upward course is at an end ;
Sharp icy *scracts* chill our ardent hopes,
  And right across from rock to rock extend
A frozen chaos of the true sublime,
Where mortal foot has never dared to climb !

LXXIV

Now up the Grimsel's bridle path we ride,
  By many a zigzag, waterworn and bare ;
Each hundred feet new scenes, as may betide,
  Disclosing to the eye, more wondrous fair ;
And now we stand upon the watershed
'Twixt Rhone and Rhine, and look down either bed.

LXXV

The mountains here, no longer robed in snow,
  Look threadbare, out at elbow, and in tags ;
The ermine cloaks which they in spring could show
  Are melted off their backs, and worn to rags ;
And each black summit, by the heat oppressed,
Sighs for more sun to cool it down to rest.

LXXVI

The glaciers only bear the tear and wear
  Of rain and sunshine in potential mood,
Where none but best of Alpine clubmen dare
  Upon their sacred solitude intrude ;
Trickling their post-meridian streamlets down
To irrigate the fields of some low town.

LXXVII

Even on the glaciers there has been a run !
  Far up the mountains many stand at rest ;
The daily drainage of a fervent sun
  Has put their solvency unto the test.
Their floating capital, the snow, is spent,
So of their hard ice they must now *take tent.*

LXXVIII

Scant is the vegetation on the way,
  For hardy rhododendrons even too high ;
Huge rugged rocks of naked granite—grey,
  And gneiss, and granite mountains jag the sky ;
Whilst through their deep ravines the foaming Aar
Tumbles and rumbles in perpetual war.

LXXIX

Now lost in some dark fathomless abyss,
  Cutting a channel that excites our wonder ;
No avalanche nor landslip comes amiss ;
  Now dashing o'er some precipice like thunder,
As if it mingled with the air, and never
Could reappear a liquid running river.

LXXX

Bold was the engineer that made the path,
  Blasting whole galleries through solid schist;
Opening a thoroughfare through such a strath,
  O'er hanging torrents, lost in clouds of mist;
Bold is the rider that can sit his horse,
Nor feel his senses reel upon the course.

LXXXI

But here the Aar becomes itself again
  After a thousand falls, and toils, and troubles,
And reappears amidst the haunts of men,
  And placidly into Brienz Lake bubbles,
And there we'll leave it to a soft repose
And bring this rugged Canto to a close.

LXXXII

Steamy and hot is Meirengen at best,
  No place to halt in in such tepid weather;
Unless to pack anew, or take a rest,
  And shape a new route, how and when and whither.
The town itself is somewhat shilly-shally,
And time is lost therein to dilly-dally.

LXXXIII

Up with the cock we rose, and had our coffee,
  And mounted Rosinante hurry-scurry,
Reserving for the steep a bit of toffee,
  Resolved to take it easy, without hurry,
And gained the plateau as the rising sun
In rosy raiment robed the mountains dun.

LXXXIV

Whilst far below Brienz lake slumbered still,
  And far above white shone the Wetterhorn ;
Whilst transcendental pine trees clothed each hill,
  And crystal dewdrops hung on birch and thorn ;
With marmots piping loud their morning call,
Where rainbow arches spanned each waterfall.

LXXXV

Now Rosenlauie's Gasthaus we have won,
  And won the jolly breakfast set before us ;
The table planted in the welcome sun,
  With stately silver fir trees waiting o'er us,
And landscapes spread before the wond'ring eye
That human pen and pencil quite defy.

LXXXVI

This rhododendron, simple flower,
  We plucked upon the pass,
Where naked needles fearful tower
  Above a *Mer de Glace* ;
Within the drifting sleety cloud,
  While snow-flakes silent fell,
And ice-fed torrents roaring loud
  Foamed hidden in each dell.

LXXXVII

Fit emblem of life's fickle fate ;
  Good guide 'neath Fortune's frown ;
It bloomed as sweet 'mid snow and slate
  As on a sunny down.

Should unkind Fortune ever gloom,
    Think then upon this flower ;
And may thy virtue guard thy bloom
    As in thy happiest hour.

CANTO SECOND

I

Twin sister of Geneva ! There you sit
   Upon the margin of thy inland sea,
In majesty a queen ! as is most fit,
   And one of the superlative degree ;
Watching thy Reuss depart to join the Rhine,
Broad, deep, majestic, tranquil, crystalline.

II

Fit contribution to thy Vaterland,
   Fit partner for the Vor and Hinter Rhine ;
A trio that compose its *fluss* so grand,
   There worshipped as a thing almost divine !
From Basle to Rotterdam, uniting all
Its Rhenish cities, whether great or small.

III

Fit resting-place, Lucerne ! thy Sweitzerhoft
   Opens its doors to tourists of all nations ;
Three hundred guests a day their doublets doff,
   And round its tables-d'hôte take up their stations,
Speaking a polyglot of every tongue,
From John O'Groat's to Burmah and Shantung.

IV

Linked to the railway world, thy public weal
  Is in a thriving and advanced condition ;
Thy public buildings to good sense appeal,
  With best of building-stone in thy possession ;
Thy new bridge is a model of its kind,
Thy old one throws us back time out of mind.

V

With warmest welcome though you tourists greet,
  Short is their sojourn in thy thriving city ;
Their exit's ready by thy Dampschiff fleet,
  And soon all scamper off devoid of pity ;
So up the lake we'll steam it at our ease,
And sketch some of its beauties, if you please.

VI

Of all the glories of this glorious land,
  That draws such tourist crowds from every nation,
In the sublime and picturesque and grand,
  None's finer to be found in all creation !
Where land and water at all points compete
To fill a picture-gallery complete !

VII

Four thousand feet the snowy peaks below,
  That circumvent it like a mountain wall,
Shrouded in clouds, and cooled by beds of snow,
  Lies Engelberg upon its grassy Thal,
With spacious meadow-lands and genial clime,
Humble amidst magnificence sublime.

VIII.

Mount Titlis, like a tortoise shelled with ice,
  Full fifty feet in thickness, clear as glass,
Sends down its glacier torrents in a trice
  To irrigate each plot of village grass ;
Whilst like a guardian angel, bare and riven,
Its Engelberg looks down from the mid-heaven.

IX

Perpetual forests clothe its uplands vast,
  The pine competing with its rival beech ;
Each tree quite fit to make a frigate's mast ;
  New seedlings rising in the shade of each.
Protected by the best of forest laws,
Recorded in the State-books every clause.

X

A strict monopoly the Senate holds
  Of all the timber on its thousand hills ;
It plants, and cuts, and sells its forest wolds ;
  No tree is felled unless the Senate wills.
Its forest-rangers watch o'er every wood,
And work the woodlands for the public good.

XI

Each noble timber, sawed across in sections,
  Is tossed into the torrent, rudely raging,
And floated down, free from all raft connexions,
  Into the lake ; the boatmen there engaging
To fish them out and land them on the shore,
And pile them up for service in great store.

XII

Nor do all segments reach the goal intended ;
 The stream of life is aptly there pourtrayed ;
Rough is the passage to the most befriended ;
 Many the kicks and knocks that must be paid.
Many are hoisted high upon the rocks,
And some get jammed between twin granite blocks.

XIII

Many are shipwrecked on the shingly strand ;
 Some are from stem to stern asunder torn ;
Numbers lie logged upon some hidden sand ;
 Some whirl in deep pools in hope forlorn ;
And when the race is run, the tear and wear
Of every fragment make the stranger stare.

XIV

All's pastoral within this valley wide ;
 The very streams are pastoral, and gush
From out each rugged marble mountain side
 As if by miracle ; and downwards rush
In gelid streamlets through the flowery meads,
Where'er the thirsty soil has greatest needs.

XV

Each chalet occupies almost a rood
 In length and breadth ; of wonderful dimensions
The roof of shingle, and the walls of wood,
 On every side with curious extensions ;
The lower story sacred to the kine,
A tribe of goats, perhaps a brood of swine.

XVI

Whilst o'er their heads the family preside,
   Midst pots, and pans, and churns, and milking pails ;
And from the rafters hang on every side,
   Scythes, hatchets, pitchforks, baskets, rakes, and rails ;
And piles of wood, for building or for burning,
Lie round the tenement at every turning.

XVII

Far up the mountains now the herds are grazing
   Upon the very verge of vegetation,
Where yesternight we saw the bonfires blazing ;
   And there all summer they must keep their station,
And work their dairies to the best account
To meet the rental to the full amount.

XVIII

No vines or fruit-trees claim the peasant's care ;
   Nor wheat nor oats exist, of frost in fear ;
But grass and grass alone luxuriates there,
   Yielding abundant hay-crops thrice a-year.
All stowed away in chalets, shingled over,
Eschewing hay-stacks with their flimsy cover.

XIX

One crop is garnered ; one's before the scythe ;
   The third October pays, though with a grudge,
When all the well-fed upland herds so *blythe*
   Descend unto the vale by many a trudge,
And crop the stubble to the very ground,
Till winter drives them all into the pound.

XX

Strict Catholics each man,—at least each woman ;
　　Hieing to mass both mid-day, even, and morn,
With festas once or twice a week, when no man
　　Dare swing a scythe without incurring scorn ;
For as the church-bells sound throughout the Thal,
Both men and women straight obey the call.

XXI

That spacious church, that palace, and that square
　　Of stately halls, o'erspreading many roods,
Is sacred to the Benedictines there,
　　Who own the valley and each household's goods.
Pity they could not mind their public ways,
And give some slender grounds for public praise.

XXII

High on the Rigi-Scheideck now we stand,
　　Upon an autumn morning crisp and clear,
And watch the sun rise o'er the Alps so grand,
　　Tinting each mountain summit far and near.
From Todi, Titlis, Uristock, Jungfrau,
Even to the minor peaks around Gersau.

XXIII

Three thousand feet below the lake still slumbers,
　　Without a breath to ruffle its smooth tide ;
And though the pines appear in countless numbers,
　　Each tree's reflected in its leafy pride ;
Each rock and chalet, landslip and cascade,
Repeats itself below in light and shade.

XXIV

The matin chimes of Gersau, now ascending,
 Mingle their music with the cattle bells ;
Broad streaks of mist, across the cliffs extending,
 Fair weather for the day at least foretells ;
And here and there a peak with broken crown
Peers through the mist, still robed in its night-gown.

XXV

A solemn stillness fills the morning air ;
 No city hums, nor carriage rattles here ;
Not even a sparrow or a crow can dare
 To chirp or caw, at least they don't appear ;
The common house-fly, ever on the wing,
Is the most noisy sort of living thing.

XXVI

An amphitheatre of Alps around us
 Circles the landscape like a picture-frame ;
With middle ground of peaks that quite astound us,
 All worthy of, but many without name,
Dappled with Alpine cedars, darkest green,
Complete the subjects of this glorious scene.

XXVII

Great was the enterprise that founded here
 A sanitarium of such vast dimensions ;
Where by the thousand, invalids each year
 May gain fresh health. and live without pretensions
Where travellers may rest in lofty ease,
And join the throng or not, just as they please.

XXVIII

And have their glass of milk three times a day,
   Warm from the cow or goat, each to his taste ;
Turning to best account their three weeks' stay ;
   Eschewing hydropathics, as mere waste
Of time and money, even of general health,
No matter what their station or their wealth.

XXIX

Above the scorching heat that teems below,
   The climate now is certainly perfection;
Fresh breezes all day long delight to blow,
   Above the reach of fever or infection.
With all appliances and means in plenty
For full enjoyment of the *far niente*.

XXX

Another day, and yet another scene !
   Another panorama spreads in sight ;
The aneroid has fallen, the hills so green
   Look nearer than their wont, and, wondrous bright,
The far-off Jungfrau never looked so near ;
Its new fallen snow-wreaths never looked so clear.

XXXI

Light fleecy clouds now wander to and fro,
   From steep to steep like broken squadrons flying,
And rally in the valleys far below,
   Rank upon rank, each other overlying.
Just like some mighty hosts prepared for battle,
With flaming rockets and the cannons' rattle.

XXXII

The wind now blows in gusts, unhatting all
  Who careless saunter on the paths on high ;
Whisking the plaster from each rubble wall,
  Dashing the gravel into every eye ;
And now the lake, with its cerulean blue,
Is overlaid with clouds and lost to view.

XXXIII

A lake of mist, and fog, and downy cloud !
  A dead sea ! motionless as you descry it ;
Spread with a coverlet or funeral shroud,
  Condemned to death as by Almighty *fiat*.
Or, like a glacier sparkling in the sun,
Before its deliquescence has begun.

XXXIV

And now at last there is a great commotion ;
  The surging misty mass is rent asunder ;
Forked lightning flashes o'er the murky ocean,—
  Our rooftree shakes with heavy peals of thunder ;
Whilst angry demons, spirits of the storm,
Appear amongst the clouds of every form.

XXXV

Towering and lowering in strange transformation,
  Now like some well-known faces 'mongst ourselves,
Their aspects changing as they change their station,
  Now like to gods of war, or monster elves ;
Now throwing off all marks of living creatures,
Now reappearing in new forms and features.

XXXVI

Tremendous is the heavenly cannonade,
  With gaping ghostly wounds a mile in length,
By 'first intention' healing, as is said,
  The wounded straight restored to health and strength;
And many a mountain, looking on the scene,
Is scathed by rending thunderbolts, we ween.

XXXVII

Now up the conflict rages, might and main,
  Enveloping the top in densest fog,
Pouring down torrents of a drenching rain,
  Soaking the grass-plots through like any bog.
No man nor beast can stand in such a storm,
But settle down like hares, each in his form.

XXXVIII

Nor ceased the hurricane for hours to flare,
  The thunder rolling in incessant roar,
The lightning blinding with excessive glare,
  Making the boldest keep within the door.
And when each guest retired to his room,
The storm still raged, still dismal was the gloom.

XXXIX

Behold the scar upon that mountain's brow,
  As if an avalanche descended there,
An avalanche of earth and stones, we trow,
  Beneath these rocky hillocks, rough and bare.
The village Goldau one rude even was found
Buried some fathoms deep beneath the ground.

D

XL.

Happy they housed their stock, both young and old,
    Whilst by the run the mountain-side came down
In one tremendous rush, as we are told,
    And buried in its ruins the whole town.
Short was their shrift, and mournful was their doom,
The house each lived in had become his tomb !

XLI

Together lived they and together died,
    Their wives and children and their babes unborn,
With all their parish feuds and petty pride,
    Their household goods, their cattle and their corn ;
Their mourners, all the peasants of the strath
As often as they chance to take that path.

XLII

And after dark no damsel can be found
    For love or money to approach the spot,
Strange cries are said to issue from the ground,
    Blue lights to glimmer under a black pot,
And weird-like forms in winding-sheets are seen
Passing from mound to mound across the green.

XLIII

Up amongst the mountain-chains,
    Above the clouds so lazy
That slumber on the humble plains
    So scorching, hot, and hazy,

Where the wild thyme the Sambur crops
    In dells that would amaze ye,
And 'mongst the cliffs the chamois hops
    At heights that drive one crazy.

XLIV

Here health and strength run hand in hand
    In open air so bracing,
Each rosy cheek and manly band,
    The sunny hillsides gracing.
Here man rejoices in his strength,
    And woman in her beauty,
And keep dull care at full arm's length,
    And bid adieu to duty.

XLV

No languor rusts the springs of life
    But time is all enjoyment,
The greatest stranger here is strife,
    Delights in full employment.
The invalid here finds a cure
    For every ailment human,
Renews his hope of life secure,
    And finds himself a new man.

XLVI

Our oldest enemy, the sun,
    Has here no power to harm us,
Though vertical his beams down run,
    Through azure skies to warm us.

But all day long we stroll about
    In shade of *sola topee*,
And pity those who groan and shout
    Below, all grimed and soapy.

XLVII

Then bundle up and leave your drill,
    Come up to Hufi's mountains,
And drink of Helicon your fill
    From Hygienic fountains.
'Mid Alpine scenery sublime
    As o'er the hills you roam
You'll here enjoy your northern clime
    And think yourself at home.

XLVIII

Once more upon the water, azure blue,
    Through Uri's lake we steam our gentle way,
With Bristenstock and Uristock in view,
    Towering aloft o'er minor sons of clay,
'Mid scenes all sacred unto William Tell,
Whom Freedom and Helvetia love so well.

XLIX

Fit birth-place for a hero of renown !
    Fit cradle for a nation's independence !
Fit graveyard for a foreign tyrant's crown !
    Fit monument of most sublime transcendance !
In Switzerland you'll nothing grander spy
Than that same landscape now before the eye.

L

Fit entrance to the pass of St. Gothard,
   Helvetia and Italia firmly binding
In mutual interest and kind regard,
   And of their duties each to each reminding
Where fifty years ago the laden mule
And laden porter was the general rule.

LI

Now lumbering waggons climb the Alpine steep
   O'er roads constructed with consummate skill,
And smart mail coaches make the transit cheap
   By easy gradients, scarping every hill,
O'er cliffs where once the goatherd feared to tread,
Where even the chamois dared not show his head.

LII

Where nought found passage but the thundering Reuss,
   O'er gneiss and granite rocky reefs descending,
Or morning cloud, or cowherd's echoing voice,
   Or avalanche or landslip, long impending,
When in a fit you'll call extremely civil,
A bridge of stone was made there by the devil.

LIII

But being rather narrow in dimensions,
   And not quite up to modern engineering,
A new one, o'er the old, of grand pretensions,
   The Austrian engineers made, nothing fearing,
Tunnelled the Devil's Stone and bored a way
Right through to Urseren, that Vale of Hay !

LIV

Time was when this broad valley was a *Sea*,
  With icebergs of all shapes and sizes floating,
Like pre-historic Saurians at play,
  Each on a field of table ice a-boating
Whilst giant pine trees stood around the shore,
With glacier cataracts in constant roar.

LV

No pine trees now grow there, nor verdant wood ;
  The hostile hordes encamped upon the plain
Cut them all down, to cook their daily food,
  Or warm their bivouacs amongst the slain.
The meddling Gauls, even here, have left their marks ;
Destructive ever like the ruthless sharks !

LVI

Now o'er the Oberalp we wind our way,
  And down the channel of the border Rhine,
'Mid scenes to which the Muse has nought to say ;
  With here and there a landslip or a mine,
'Mid desolation of the raging river,
All down its stony course destructive ever.

LVII

Now whilst at Reichenau we bait the horses
  At junction of the Vor and Hinter Rhine,
Let's take a glimpse of their united forces
  Here called *par excellence* old Father Rhine !
Silent and stately now it winds along,
Deep in its waters, in its current strong !

LVIII

Here Louis Philippe, fallen from princely state,
   On slender pittance helped to keep a school,
Bending to stern necessity, yet great
   In his vocation and scholastic rule,
Learning a lesson useful by and by,
Himself a Student of Adversity.

LIX

Sure we have got to Erebus at last!
   And that must be its entrance in the mist!
And this must be the Styx! this volume vast
   Of inky water gurgling through the schist,
Polluting the pure stream of Hinter Rhine
Just like the washings-out of a coal mine.

LX

What chamois worthy of immortal fame
   First found a passage through the *Via Mala*?
Cross precipices, then unknown by name,
   Leaping from cliff to cliff and rocky *scala*,
Now jumping right across the Hinter Rhine,
Now bridging o'er it on a prostrate pine?

LXI

We know the engineer renowned in story,
   Who scarped and tunnelled the entire way,
A work immense and of surpassing glory,
   The roadway marvel of this touring day.
A real triumph for a Kaisar's crown,
Redounding much to Austrian renown!

LXII

Here ! cliff on cliff, like steps of a stone stair,
  Conduct the eye into the vault of heaven.
There ! rocks like ruined walls, all cracked and bare,
  Shattered by earthquakes, and by lightning riven,
Hang overhead, portending some disaster,
And drive the coachman to whip by the faster.

LXIII

A hundred yards sheer down beneath our feet
  The river rages with terrific force,
The precipices almost seem to meet,   [course,
  And here and there, trapped in their downward
Large fragments hang suspended in the air,
Forming rude bridges of construction rare.

LXIV

Gigantic pine trees straight as spear shafts rise,
  Root over top in every deep ravine,
Until their branches vanish in the skies,
  Whilst here and there one prostrate may be seen,
Stretching across the channel of the river,
To foot which, even in thought, excites a shiver.

LXV

Few heads can stand the transit cross the ridges,
  The seat upon the box feels insecure,
The risk seems great of falling off the bridges,
  And what a fall would that be to be sure !
Here clever little urchins throw down stones
To show what chance there would be for one's bones.

LXVI

Now two long weary hours we've upwards trod
    The great Augustan military way,
Treading perhaps in fact, the selfsame sod
    Which Julius Cæsar did in former day,
When ruthless Rome her legions northwards hurled
To conquer and enslave the northern world.

LXVII

Two rude stone columns mark the Juliers Pent,
    Where meet the waters of the Inn and Rhine,
Erected to narrate some great event
    Which even in history has ceased to shine,
The whole inscription every letter lost,
By Time's disintegration, and by frost.

LXVIII

Sole vestige on the pass of days of yore,
    Of Roman glory, or of Gothic shame,
Dull, dateless monuments, none can restore,
    Unfaithful cenotaphs without a name !
Where tens of thousands met and fought and fled,
Or on the gory rocks made their death bed !

LXIX

Oh what a panorama's now in sight !
    To paint that landscape would require a score
Of artists, academic in their might,
    With canvas large as a cathedral door,
Where snowy Alpine peaks and passes vie
And boundless glaciers on their bosoms lie.

LXX

Behold the Engadine spread out before us
   Like a rich carpet of a Persian dye,
With pine-clad precipices rising o'er us,
   And meadows, lakes, and forests 'neath the eye,
Through which the infant Inn begins its life,
Tranquil and clear, ere it begins its strife.

LXXI

Crisp is the air, for this the end of June !
   Fast falls the snow ! the sun shines cold and clear,
The winter's scarcely over ! All too soon !
   Bright Flora threw her garlands o'er its bier,
Her early blossoms opened but to die,
And on the scanty grass abortive lie.

LXXII

Now July's come ! the favourite of the year;
   Fresh flowers have bloomed anew, o'er hill and dale.
Each hillock is a bouquet to revere,
   No lady could put down her finger nail
Without disturbing some pure gem in flower,
Fit for a bridal nosegay, or a bower.

LXXIII

Now all the insect life is on the wing !
   And all the touring world is on the run !
Drinking cold draughts from each chalybeate spring,
   Or basking in the rays of the warm sun,
The more athletic scaling snowy peaks,
With health and vigour beaming on their cheeks !

LXXIV

Now August wanes : the Inn begins to fall,
   The three short summer months are nearly over,
The ice-fed rivulets have ceased to brawl,
   And new-fallen snow the middling mountains cover.
Hoar frost lies white upon the morning sward,
And martins southward flown, have left their card.

LXXV

The dying summer, like the dolphin dying,
   Becomes more beautiful in its decay,
Its gorgeous tints the pen and brush defying,
   To paint their semblance at the close of day,
More heavenly seems the landscape to the view,
Blending into the sky each rosy hue !

LXXVI

September's come, with pinching cold and sleet !
   Deep wreaths of snow lie white on every mountain;
The pines are dressed, each in its winding sheet.
   And sealed up for the winter is each fountain ;
To warmer climes the visitors now fly,
Leaving the year to linger out and die.

LXXVII

Bright shines the rising sun o'er Pontresina,
   Tinting each mountain cheek with warmer hue ;
Sharp blows the morning breeze from the Bernina,
   Whilst sparkle on the turf big drops of dew,
With many a naked peak and glacier green
Along the roadway mingling in the scene.

LXXVIII

Familiar friends ! though cold and distant all ;
　Chilling advances and sincere devotions,
Treating their visitors at morning call
　To freezing mixtures and odd icy *notions*,
Though somewhat slippery to a stranger's eye,
Most firm in substance and integrity!

LXXIX

Second to none amongst the Alpine chains
　The great Bernina looms in stately pride ;
A dozen minor peaks the Chief retains,
　Each sending down a glacier from its side,
Few grander feats our Alpine clubmen try
Than Piz-Bernina, now before the eye !

LXXX

'Twas only yesterday a pair returned
　Successful in their climb, with footsteps slow,
All feather-bed indulgences they spurned,
　And slept till midnight hutted on the snow,
Then lighting torches, axed their icy way,
And reached the summit at the break of day.

LXXXI

In time to see each star, revered in story,
　Withdrawing from the sky and lost to view,
In time to see the sun in morning glory
　Rise from a cloudless bed of ruby blue,
Gilding with Orient light each rugged peak,
And turning earth to heaven in silence meek.

LXXXII

Black, bare, and barren is the watershed
　　Between the rivers of the Inn and Po,
Not even a heathbell here can find a bed,
　　And nought but ugly stones appear to grow,
Rough and gigantic from some earthquake's throes
Born but to lie in profitless repose.

LXXXIII

Here meet the feeders of two mighty seas—
　　The Adriatic and its Euxine brother ;
And with a glass of water, as you please,
　　You may pay tribute to the one or other,
And have your off'ring paid with all devotion,
Or in the Black Sea, or Venetia's Ocean.

LXXXIV

There starts a torrent from Cambrina's side,
　　Cuirassed with solid ice like coat of mail,
Massing its waters n that milky tide,
　　And gathering strength to leap down to the vale
O'er rock and precipice in headlong speed,
To Poschiavo and its flowery mead.

LXXXV

Now let us cast aloft our wond'ring eyes
　　Upon the Palu Glacier in its might,
Like a huge river falling from the skies,
　　All frozen hard and fast as by a sprite,
Up which the foot of man has never trod,
Yet leading man from earth below to God !

LXXXVI

Now on the Grand-Alp Grum we take our stand,
　　And look down on the vales of Italie
Spread out as by some weird enchanter's wand,
　　With all its beauty and fertility,
The landscape ever changing, ever new!
Steeped in an atmosphere of hazy blue.

LXXXVII

This little lake, embosomed in the hills,
　　Is Poschiavo called.   The inn ' Le Prese,'
Fed by the Poschi-Vino and some rills
　　That well from limestone rocks, all cracked and crazy,
Here Autumn with mild weather lingers still,
And here we'll halt, and run up a long bill.

LXXXVIII

The walnut and the chestnut side by side,
　　Luxuriate here in bountiful redundance,
And pumpkins, large as beehives, form the pride
　　Of every matron in their rich abundance;
Whilst goats and cattle fill the milking pail,
And Want in any form here tells no tale.

LXXXIX

Loud but monotonous the herdsman's horn
　　Summons his hairy flock at break of day.
Cool and congenial is the dewy morn,
　　And sweetly smell the meads of tedded hay;
The rendezvous is at the village gate,
Where soon by twos and threes the goats await.

XC

Thence after muster, Damon in the van
    Leads them to browsing ground, amongst the rocks :
And when the day is over at a scan,
    Their pastor leads them home, right well-fed flocks,
Each threading its own way to its own home,
And woe betide it if it do not come.

XCI

The guide-books say the lake is filled with trout,
    But angling we have found a mere delusion,
And felt the pith of Dr Johnson's knout,
    And put away our tackle in confusion ;
Fishing abroad we've found but sorry sport
At best, and seldom worth one's while in short.   \

XCII

Now up the Adda and the Valtelline,
    Through orchards, vines, and corn-fields on each hand,
Famed for the quality of its red wine,
    The vintage sixty-eight the choicest brand :
The river raging like a thing of life
Tearing its banks to pieces, in its strife.

XCIII

Sweeping away whole cottages and trees
    Like straws upon its torrent hardly seen,
Depositing whole islands by degrees,
    Now sweeping one away from out the scene,
Hurling along its bottom mighty stones
That make their torture heard by mighty groans.

XCIV

Once on a time it made a fatal blunder,
  And undermined a mountain in its wrath,
A landslip bringing down with noise like thunder
  And damming up its course, across the strath,
Turning the fertile valley to a lake,
And deluging each châlet, field, and brake.

XCV

Peasants are living still within the vale,
  Who witnessed the calamity appalled,
Who saw the water rise, the flood prevail,
  And man and beast escaping ere enthralled;
Who saw the Adda burst its dam apace,
And reassume its rocky normal race.

XCVI

Those grotesque hillocks mark the fatal spot
  Where cot and cottager were overthrown :
A barren and an unproductive lot,
  With brambles, thorns and thistles overgrown,
Which keep the peasantry in constant dread,
Lest some such fate should fall upon their head.

XCVII

Thus have we seen, upon life's chequered path,
  A wife enamoured of domestic war
Bring down upon her head her husband's wrath,
  Who shut her up behind both bolt and bar,
Till penitence and penance made her civil,
And saved the shrew from running to the devil.

CANTO THIRD

I

THERE like some swallows-nests against the rocks
Precipitous and bare, against all laws,
Where scarcely even a wiry wary fox
Could find a footing for his pawky paws—
Are built the baths of Bormio, hot and cold,
Both large establishments, a new and old !

II

There vegetation ends and rocks arise,
Steep, stern, and tattered, towering o'er the scene !
Rearing their shattered summits to the skies
And pouring down dry shingle in their spleen ;
The only soil found there, dry as a whistle !
Fit only for a nettle or a thistle !

III

Yet human beings in their deep distress,
In their despair, more genial places failing,
Assemble there in scores, and seek redress,
From ev'ry mental care and carnal ailing.
Finding relief perhaps for their dry bones,
Sermons and sage advice from these dry stones.

E

IV

You'd think the world here came to an end,
    And that these mountain walls were insurmountable;
But lo ! the zig-zags up the shingle trend,
    And soon you'll find their numbers quite uncountable;
There where the wind blows through it like a funnel,
The Stelvio pass commences by a tunnel.

V

There comes the Adda down the pass careering,
    Tumultuous more than ever in its bearing.
Nought's like a river for good engineering,
    A passage through the limestone slowly wearing.
Without the Adda, Austria's engineer
Had tried in vain to make the passage clear.

VI

Let's call a halt ! and let us view unfurled
    These Alpine wonders, this stupendous scene !
The ruins of an earthquake ! of a world !
    Mountain on mountain piled to heaven serene,
Beyond the tread of mortal man to climb,
Fit footstool for Omnipotence sublime !

VII

Eight thousand feet above the sea, we stand
    Upon the northern verge of Italie,
With snowy mountains loftier, on each hand,
    And wondrous glaciers sparkling brilliantly
Where the thin air makes hard the respiration,
To keep the system equal to the occasion.

VIII

There Mount Crystallo sentinels the pass,
    Stupendous in its altitude and size;
Sheeted in ice as clear and clean as glass,
    From which the infant Adda takes its rise,
With Ortler higher still, enormous mass!
Sending huge glaciers down through each crevass.

IX

No pines nor oaks, no chestnuts, and no yews
    Can make a living in this blasted region!
Even junipers, and ferns, and heaths refuse
    To show a leaf amongst these stony legions;
Mosses and lichens that can live on stone
Of all the vegetable kingdom thrive alone!

X

The marmot's lord of the creation here!
    Now busy storing for his winter quarters;
And that's his whistle, piping shrill and clear,
    Warning his youngsters to beware of Tartars.
And that's an avalanche at which you wonder,
Rumbling exactly like a clap of thunder.

XI

These waterfowl that southwards swiftly fly
    Are birds of passage, just like you and me,
In quest of sunny climes and azure sky,
    And from a winter snell are glad to flee.
And there, just like a brigand in the skies,
The Lammergeyer marks them for a prize!

XII

These classic sheep, with their big Roman noses,
　Nibbling their way amongst the barren rocks,
Are homeward steering, now the summer closes,
　From their Transalpine pastures, well-fed flocks,
To their liege lords in Lombardy so flat,
Laden with snowy fleeces and with fat.

XIII

Let us descend the Old Etrurian way,
　The route of Roman armies northwards marching,
The route of Huns and Goths of antique lay,
　Descending from the Alps, for plunder searching ;
Steep and zig-zaggy is its best condition ;
Here one false footstep leads unto perdition.

XIV

Some miles below appears a loaded waggon,
　Drawn by a string of horses, mules, and asses ;
And how the summit they're to get a bag on,
　Our comprehension certainly surpasses.
Yet there a railway is proposed to run,
Its survey in good earnest is begun.

XV

These two green grassy mounds upon the road
　Were once the strongholds of the ancient way,
Where Roman myrmidons transfixed each load,
　And black mail made the northern traders pay.
Save these no vestige, not one single stone,
Remains to chronicle the days long gone !

XVI

But Nature, faithful to her own creation,
   Has propagated yearly every flower,
As perfect as of yore blooms the carnation,
   The wild thyme's scent is perfect to this hour.
But races that once filled the rolls of fame
Have fled like smoke, and left nought but a name !

XVII

Past Franzenshöhe, Mondatch and Trafoi,
   We rattled down by many a zigzag mile,
Halting an hour or more at Gamagoi,
   An Austrian fort, commanding the defile,
And in the evening took a quiet stroll
Amidst the fertile fields of the Tyrol.

XVIII

That is the great Adige's mighty flood,
   Now almost to a standstill daily bled,
By each possessor of some fertile rood,
   And here and there found dead upon its bed,
But which (its tribute water duly paid),
No hostile host would ford in fellest raid.

XIX

Here railway engineers now lead their forces,
   On from Cisalpine through Transalpine Gaul,
Right through the mountains charge their iron horses,
   Ravine or precipice them nought appal ;
And when the rail is laid, proud men they may be,
And may a crown of gold their mead that day be.

XX

Land of the vine, the olive, and the maize!
  Where Ceres and Pomona in rotation
Have spread a feast meet for an angel's praise,
  And man and beast cram full each habitation,
Where melons, pumpkins, gourds of every shape,
Vie with the nectarine, the peach, and grape.

XXI

Where with an ill-assorted feeble team,
  A horse and steer—a donkey and a mule,
Yoked to a ploughshare, rude in the extreme,
  The earth is furrowed by old Saturn's rule,
And sprinkled o'er with corn seed as of old,
Returning to the farm a hundred fold.

XXII

The landscape far and wide with vines is shaded,
  Spread upon trellis-work in vast profusion,
The purple clusters seem for sale paraded,
  No check to strangers' prying, or intrusion.
One feels uneasy lest some slender twig
Should snap, and drop a bunch upon one's wig.

XXIII

Here invalids from every northern clime
  Resort to eat fresh grapes, and try their cure,
And find Meran delightful for the time,
  Their ailments there made easy to endure,
And driving them without ere rhyme or reason
To take their chambers for next autumn's season.

XXIV

Now down to Botzen at an easy pace,
    Red porphyritic rocks we drive among,
(Thought precious stones by the old Roman race,
    And still by moderns bought at prices long).
Where slabs are quarried large as mess-room tables,
With which they pave their streets, or slate their stables.

XXV

There are the famous Dolomitic mountains!
    Sawing the skies! all sharp and bleak and bare,
Unseen their herbage, and unheard their fountains,
    With which none but Mount Sinai can compare.
Crumbling to sand and gravel year by year,
And spreading rounding their base a desert drear.

XXVI

Bolzano has a climate quite Italian!
    Vines in the valleys, pine trees on the hills,
With wines in wood, to please a Bacchanalian,
    And sawing, silk, and cotton water-mills,
The dialect a bastard sort of branch
Of ancient Latin, known as the Romansch.

XXVII

Language, like man, is doomed to live and die;
    Its span of life is scarce one thousand years;
Letters and words evanish from the eye,
    Like mortal men, along this vale of tears;
And Trajan, were he raised from his long home,
Would not be understood in modern Rome.

XXVIII

German by name, Italian as a nation,
  Botzen's an enterprising thriving city,
With streams of water running through each station,
  And handsome husbandmen, and women pretty,
Each thinks his lot in pleasant places cast,
And finds this year as happy as the last.

XXIX

Lago di Garda ! Riva ! Peschiera !
  What stirring thoughts around your names arise,
For there the gallant hero of Caprera,
  Hoisted the tricolore unto the skies,
And with his red shirts and some Bersaglieri
Flustered the Kaisar's eagles in their eyrie !

XXX

Stern is the scene, yet picturesque withal,
  The mountains misty, muddy every rill ;
Yet sunny tints of freedom on them fall,
  Glimpses of liberty on lake and hill,
Where late oppression ruled with rods of steel,
And Austrian tyrants trod with iron heel.

XXXI

There stands the stronghold of the Kaisar's crown,
  His eagles flown ! The tricolore upon it !
Italian sentries pacing up and down,
  Italian bugles sounding call or sonnet,
And that is Solferino, in the distance !
Which put an end to Austrian resistance.

XXXII

And gave Italia back her better half,
   Thanks to the French, who took a potent part,
And with their warlike emperor and staff,
   Entered the lists and fought with hand and heart.
And from the Alps unto the Adriatic,
Declared Italia free ! in phrase dramatic !

XXXIII

Red ran the Mincio on that desperate day,
   The thirsty soil was puddled with their blood,
And there, if careful search be made, you may
   Pick up some trophy, buried in the mud,
An eagle's claw, a thaler, or a franc,
A horse-shoe, or a bullet, or a crank.

XXXIV

Shakespeare's Verona ! venerable city !
   Home of Catullus ! of Paul Veronese !
Of Romeo and Juliet ! once so witty !
   In state and circumstances once so easy !
Where Roman emperors once held their court,
Of Dante, Guido, Titian, the resort !

XXXV

How art thou fallen from thy imperial state !
   When Diocletian built thy Colosseum
Still standing ! still defying time and fate !
   The world's wonder still ! a vast museum !
Humble and lowly now you play your part !
Thy riches little but thy works of art !

XXXVI

Embedded in thy walls, thy frescoes stand
  Beyond the reach of rapine or of fire ;
Not even the French, so covetously grand,
  Could rob you of these treasures in their ire !
Long may they grace each nave, and aisle, and apse,
Secure from burglary and dire mishaps.

XXXVII

Thy mediæval monuments would fill
  A cemet'ry on any grave occasion ;
Thy saints and sinners if unniched at will,
  Would crowd thy Duomo as a congregation.
The paintings rotting on thy mildewed walls
Would make a floorcloth for our own St. Paul's.

XXXVIII

But now the tide has turned, and fortune's favours
  Will soon be cast into your very lap.
Thy railway will assist thine own endeavours
  And you its cornucopia can tap.
You've gentlemen got still of flint and steel,
To put their shoulders stoutly to the wheel.

XXXIX

Old Padua, I cannot pass you by
  Without a stanza to your august name.
In mediæval times none stood more high,
  Or had more niches in the fanes of Fame.
For letters, sculpture, poetry, or painting,
For starry science, politics, or sainting.

XL

Thy university turned out such men
  As Tasso, Dante, Petrarch, Ariosto,
And Galileo of our planet's ken,
  And Titian, Guido, Giotto and Robusto.
And even some doges wielding lictors' fasces,
Have sat as students in thy higher classes.

XLI

And round thy Grand Piazza, like a border,
  Sculptured more large than life in bright Carrara,
Thy leading prizemen stand in open order,
  Like sentinels on service in Mercara.
Holding distinction up to public view,
And from the world receiving honours due.

XLII

But Fame's a lottery ! as well as life !
  Merit is not enough to rise to Fame !
What multitudes of Great Men in their strife,
  Are yet without a prize, without a name !
Men fit to rank with Poussin or Guercino,
With Claude, Canova, or Domenichino.

XLIII

St. Anthony was native of thy town,
  And blessed thy beasts of burden once a year.
And wrought strange miracles of high renown,
  And underwent his great Temptation here.
When Satan tried to bribe him, like a fool !
To drop his cowl, and join his wicked school.

XLIV

What strange sensation moves St. Marco's Square?
    Has some new island risen from the main?
Has Commerce raised her right hand in the air,
    And sworn 'Poor Venice shall be rich again.'
. No! Venice now rejoices in such glee,
To learn her elder sister Rome is free !

XLV

Twin sisters they! Both bore the servile yoke
    Of stern oppression in its sternest sway ;
Which galled them to the very bone, and broke
    Their proudest hearts, and sank them in dismay,
'Neath Austria's bondage Venice had to groan !
Rome could not call her very soul her own !

XLVI

Soon every shop was shut. The tricolore
    From every window, every masthead waved,
And banners in procession proudly bore
    ' Rome, capital of Italy, is saved ! '
Then every church-bell rang its merriest peal,
Till domes, and spires, and turrets seemed to reel.

XLVII

And when night dropped her mantle o'er the fray,
    Bright gas lit up the square right splendidly.
Even old St. Marco's tour, so grim and gray,
    Was made a beacon for the jubilee.
The city pigeons cooed their roundelay,
And the bronze horses almost seemed to neigh.

XLVIII

And martial music echoed round the square,
  The old and young all joining in the dances,
And many a hopeful youth and damsel fair
  With one another interchanged sweet glances :
Till midnight echoed from St. Marco's dome,
When forthwith one and all departed home.

XLIX.

Home of departed doges' royal state !
  Prosperity seems banished from thy halls !
One's very heart bleeds to perceive your fate,
  And how deserted are thy grand canals.
Silent and slow now row thy gondoliers,
And beauties from their windows look in tears.

L

The streams that formed your islands in the sea,
  Have silted up old channels with new sand :
And at low tide square miles of mud you see,
  Above salt water spread almost to land.
Now Alaric or Attila, if to the fore,
Might march their forces right across from shore.

LI

Thus the protection which the sea once gave you,
  From hostile hordes descending from the Alps,
Has passed away, and could no longer save you
  From being plundered, to your very scalps.
Then cease to place your safety on the sea,
And trust to terra firma for your *dree*.

LII

You've bridged across your shoals and your lagunes,
  And arched a railway right into your city.
You've fertilised your barren sandy dunes,
  And mowed down reeds and rushes without pity.
Now deepen thy canals, and throw the mud
Upon thy shoals, and raise them 'bove the flood.

LIII

But time will come when thy deep Adriatic
  Will be filled up with Alpine silt and sand,
When thy swift galleys, with their keels erratic,
  Will be replaced by ploughshares, on dry land.
When thy rude husbandmen will sweat and toil,
And railway trains will rattle o'er the soil.

LIV

You're not so poor as you appear to stand ;
  In every church you've untold riches got ;
Statues and paintings by old masters grand,
  Running to ruin and the dread dry rot.
Send them to auction ! and thus raise new matter
To meet thy public wants by land or water.

LV

What means this overcrowded railway station ?
  Thy citizens assembled in such haste ?
These files of soldiers armed for state occasion
  Of industry and time why so much waste ?
Has old St. Antony come back 'mongst men
To bless thy living creatures o'er again ?

LVI

Is this some festa for thy Tintoretto?
  Has some prize masterpiece of old renown
Been found concealed in rubbish in the Ghetto,
  And as a gift been sent unto thy town?
Has stern old Shylock reappeared afresh
And of Antonio claimed his pound of flesh?

LVII

Who are those men that fill each railway car,
  Of dashing uniform and comely mien?
Rueful and sad, like prisoners of war?
  The marked performers of this bustling scene!
Silent they came, without a single cheer!
Silent they go, without a single jeer!

LVIII

These are the Papal myrmidons of Rome,
  That fenced the Papa in St. Peter's chair;
Disbanded now, and hence returning home,
  With due respect, free from expense or care.
These are the men of infamous renown,
Who trod the Romans and their freedom down!

LIX

Lost in the lapse of centuries forgot,
  Unknown thy birthday! dateless thy first home,
Rising and falling with Etruscan lot,
  The friend of Hannibal! the foe of Rome!
Surviving races buried underground,
Still standest thou, Bologna, safe and sound!

LX

The Alma Mater of the world of letters !
   The nurse of arts and sciences sublime !
Thy university tore off the fetters
   That chained humanity to dotard time.
And mediæval rubbish cleared away,
And o'er its dark paths threw the light of day.

LXI

' The proper study of mankind '—of Man !
   Was first elucidated in thy school,
His mechanism witnessed at a scan,
   Fearful and wonderful his vital rule !
And here Galvani of transcendent fame
Found out the vital spark that bears his name.

LXII

And here the softer sex, themselves unsexing,
   Once lectures read and filled professors' chairs,
Spending their thoughts on studies most perplexing,
   Devoted to their academic cares.
Bologna's famous still for men of mark,
Akin to him of the electric spark.

LXIII

Misgoverned long by cardinals unwise !
   An air of sanctity pervades you still,
Though first of Papal States to fraternise
   And join Italia's standard with good will.
Bononia, long numbered with the dead,
Begins once more to raise her sickly head.

LXIV

Go, if your time allows, and cross that brook,
  And mount that hill by its six thousand steps,
And see the virgin's portrait by St Luke !
  (Apocryphal declared by all adepts),
Just eighteen hundred years ago depicted !
In no wise as to time or truth restricted !

LXV

But it has been confirmed by Papal bull,
  And consecrated as a holy relique.
A modest fresco of uncertain school,
  And set in gold and precious stones, angelic,
The altar-piece of the *chiesa* proud !
The adoration of a pilgrim crowd !

LXVI

The cost of church and colonnades immense
  Staggers all calculation as to sum,
One wonders what became of common sense,
  And from what quarters so much gold could come ;
Enough to build anew your University
Squandered away by bigoted perversity !

LXVII

Now up the Apennines, with panting steed,
  Through endless tunnels and o'er lofty bridges.
We scale the mountains, though with slackened speed.
  Through fertile olive groves, o'er chestnut ridges.
With fair Bologna sleeping far below,
And Reno glancing in the morning glow.

LXVIII

Now we have gained, laboriously and slow,
   The highest level of the Apennine,
Five hundred feet beneath the frozen snow
   That gems Italia's waistbelt, all divine;
And rattling swiftly through a lengthy tunnel,
Emerge in open air as from a funnel.

LXIX

Refreshed with water and with wheels new greased,
   The engine whistled and each took his place,
All with the sylvan scenery well pleased,
   And slided down at an alarming pace,
Through crumbling rocks and slipping beds of clay,
The engine seeming bent to run away.

LXX

No fairer scene than this the world contains,
   With nought of the stupendous and sublime,
A gentle valley where abundance reigns,
   With medium temperature and genial clime,
Its manly people famed for art and science,
Working them both in intimate alliance !

LXXI

Etruscan Florence ! Beautiful Firenze !
   What can we say to thee not said before
In sober prose or in poetic phrenzy,
   In Greek or Latin, or in modern lore ?
A library thy history would fill,
And incomplete would leave thy records still.

LXXII

First in the van of Italy regenerate,
  Making thy clarion heard throughout the land,
You've taught Italia's sons her flag to venerate,
  And rallied 'neath thy banner every band.
Nova Italia is thy motto now,
With liberty imprinted on each brow !

LXXIII

Great Nurse of Arts and Sciences of yore ;
  You've seen them rise and fall, and rise again,
In their Renaissance ; vigorous once more
  The highest pitch of eminence attain !
Staring thy zenith like a Milky Way,
And lighting all below them in the fray.

LXXIV

Once more, Renaissance, you have made your care
  Of works municipal and common-place;
New roads, new streets, new boulevard, new square,
  New church façades, new quay, new water-race,
New homesteads given thy living and thy dead,
And to thy people given new daily bread.

LXXV

Pisa forlorn ! sunk with thy sinking tower ;
  Thy prestige and thy prospects humbled low,
Time was, when at the climax of thy power
  You held your own, returning blow for blow
With Genoa or Venice in their glory,
And filled thy towns with mediæval story.

LXXVI

Extending thy domains along the sea-board,
  Annexing islands in thy southern ocean,
Manning thy fleet with culverin and leaboard,
  Keeping both Turk and Saracen in motion,
Stretching thy commerce far beyond the seas,
And bartering for silks with the Chinese.

LXXVII

Embarking in thy port, the fierce Crusaders
  Took their departure for the Holy Land :
Filling with warrior-freight thy tall-mast traders,
  Which landed them all safe on Joppa's strand.
Returning home with *terra santa* delved
From Calvary itself, devoutly shelved

LXXVIII

In your cathedral's Campo Santo ! where
  Thy saintly sacerdotals soundly sleep,
With bright perennials blooming on each lair,
  Where bolt and bar the cemetery keep
Secure from touch or tread of unbelievers,
And desperately wicked false deceivers !

LXXIX

We've stood on Calvary, and wondered where
  So much good fertile loam was ever found ;
They must have scraped the rocks all clear and bare,
  For there we could not find one single pound !
In fact the mount was built of solid stone ;
The pseudo-rockery all right well done.

LXXX

Livorna, though thy city's but a poor one,
  Yet you have got a harbour passing fine,
Sheltered from wind and wave, a most secure one.
  Where merchantment and iron-clads of the line
May ride at anchor in the roughest weather,
Safe as a grazing nag upon a tether.

LXXXI

  Oh, Toby ! dear Toby !
  Oh how could you so be
    Perverse as to wander away
  With dog-stealing Tartars,
  And leave such fine quarters
    With such a kind master to play ?

LXXXII

  Now no one will pet you,
  Or nice mess will get you,
    Or hassock will place by the fire,
  Or join in a lark now,
  Or lead to the park now,
    Alas ! you'll have none to admire.

LXXXIII

  No fresh butcher meat now ;
  Cat's meat you must eat now;
    Your bedding of wheat, straw, or hay,
  Your master a cabby,
  Your messmate a tabby,
    Your black coat all dusty and grey.

LXXXIV

My heart is quite broken !
Of nought else I've spoken ;
    My eyes are o'erflowing with tears.
Now nought else I dream of,
No hope there's a gleam of,
    And ev'ry day adds to my fears.

LXXXV

Perhaps you've been killed
And in piecemeal been grilled,
    Or minced up for sausages fine ;
Or made into hare-soup,
Or some other rare soup,
    For gourmands who know how to dine.

LXXXVI

Your skin stuffed with tow,
In some window for show,
    Or tanned into leather for gloves,
Or made into slippers,
For light-going trippers,
    When slily they steal to their loves.

LXXXVII

Alas it should so be !
That my little Toby
    His best friends should wantonly cross ;
He'll now undeceived be,
And shockingly grieved be,
    To learn the extent of his loss. .

LXXXVIII

But dogs are like men,
Who, like nine out of ten,
    Think nothing of best boons when given ;
Till hard fate comes o'er them,
And stares straight before them,
    And finds them with heart-strings all riven.

CANTO FOURTH.

I

Now whilst we pace the poop on board the screw,
   The Nomentino! for Palermo bound,
What multitudes of *navvies* join the crew,
   Resolved to push their fortunes on new ground,
To reap the harvest of the lazy Sarde,
And carry home triumphant their reward.

II

Warm is the afternoon, and clear the heaven,
   And lucky for the *navvies* it is true,
For sitting room is all the sea-room given!
   Heaven grant it may continue all night through!
No bedding but the bare planks for their bed!
No cover but the clouds above their head!

III

Far to the west beneath the setting sun,
   See Corsica ascending to the skies!
Its mountains tipped with snow, now rose and dun,
   Which even Italian summer suns defies,
The cradle of the Great Man of the Age!
The victim of ambition, greed, and rage!

IV

And see far to the east his isle Elba !
Obscured in clouds, presaging early storm !
Whence the caged eagle flew, with beak and claw
　Resolved to fight, his empire to reform ;
And soon his gauntlet, burnished up anew,
He in the faces of his gaolers threw.

V

There come the Merry Andrews of the sea,
　A shoal of dolphins in fantastic mood,
Playing at leap-frog, tumbling in high glee,
　Like acrobats, performing for their food ;
Darting across our bows, as if the steamer,
Had gone to sleep, and had become a dreamer.

VI

Whilst like a Triton leader in persistence ;
　A spermaceti whale begins to snort
His bright parabolas, far in the distance,
　And looms just like a jolly boat, in short,
And lightning flashes 'neath the dark horizon,
On which the weather-wise all set their eyes on.

VII

Set in a stormy sky, all black and blue,
　In which the rainbow rears its broken arch,
Lit by a glimpse of sun of orient hue,
　Bleak, serrated, and bare, without one march,
Behold Caprera ! Garibaldi's isle !
His kingdom ! and his farm ! where he can smile

VIII

At statesmen's jealousy and papists' scorn,
  And live within himself, and calmly view,
Growing in vigour, Italy new born,
  True to herself! to her Dictator true!
Now independent of his sword or fiat,
Rich in prosperity, in peace, and quiet!

IX

Despising riches, honours, and rewards,
  Like Cincinnatus, there he holds his plough!
Content with his own family's regards,
  Growing his corn, and rearing goat and cow;
His only want on earth—his want of soil,
To recompense him for his sweat and toil!

X

How comes it, Roman freemen! that the man
  Who more than any other helped to make you,
Who thy forlorn-hope led, first in its van!
  Prepared to die, but never to forsake you—
How comes it you've forgot him?—ostracised him?
What base ingratitude thus to have prized him!

XI

Last night the sun went down in grief and tears,
  A drenching rain set in with a sirocco,
Blasting our hopes, confirming all our fears,
  Soon as each man had had his mug of cocoa;
And all night through it blew a heavy gale,
The rain-drops mingled now and then with hail.

XII

And once a lunar rainbow 'mid the storm
  Shone like an apparition ! ghastly pale !
Pale as a moonbeam ! fleeting in its form !
  Its segment broken by the raging gale.
While phosphorescent lights rolled in the wake,
And showed the life-buoys slung upon the *break*.

XIII

The scene this morning beat all powers of speech ;
  Five hundred *navvies* locked in one another,
Cold, wet, and sea-sick, beyond pity's reach,
  Each resting on some other, like a brother.
No wailing, no complaining, silent all !
Content to get on shore and out of thrall.

XIV

Isle of the Sarde ! the mouflon ! and wild boar !
  Of myrtle jungles and of fever swamps !
Of marble mountains, and Nuraggis hoar !
  Of thriftless huzzies, and of lazy scamps !
Familiar with the dagger and the gun ;
Too proud to work ! too stolid even for fun !

XV

Where strangers make your railways, and your roads,
  And fell your timber, and even reap your fields,
And work your quarries, and even mine your lodes,
  And mint the metal that the furnace yields,
And fill their purses with the precious metal,
And laugh to scorn thy laggards without *fettle*.

XVI

Yet nature has bestowed on you an isle
   Which might be made a garden of delight.
Where cornfields, vineyards, cottages, might smile,
   With a fine climate, healthy, breezy, bright,
Now overrun with jungle, and with reeds,
Scarce equal to its scanty people's needs!

XVII

Now snug in Cagliari we dry each feather,
   And salve our broken shins and broken noses;
Favoured by neither sun, nor moon, nor weather,
   Reposing on no beds of scented roses.
No stormier passage have we ever made;
None's nastier, in the Sicilian trade.

XVIII

For Cagliari new prospects are begun
   Of rising in prosperity and name;
From south to north a railway soon will run
   And give a fillip to its trade so lame,
Its harbour's good, and though of small dimension,
In length and breadth admits of great extension.

XIX

Corpo di Baccho !   What a drove is here
   Of fourth class passengers prepared to board!
Struck dumb with consternation and with fear,
   Their shaggy sides all bleeding, poked and gored,
Hoisted like hampers, by the horns aloft,
And dropped into the hold, all warm and soft.

XX

There lashed securely, and in right array,
  Each has his billet and his room to lie on,
Protected from the wind, and rain, and spray,
  Sea sickness all they need to keep an eye on ;
But man on board ship and upon the billows
Becomes a tyrant only to his fellows !

XXI

Last night the sun went down clear and serene,
  The moon at full relieving him of duty,
With brightest lustre lighting up the scene,
  Making each ugly cliff a thing of beauty,
Dimming the light on Spartivento's cape,
And showing every rock, its form and shape.

XXII

But ere the first watch of the night was spent.
  A fresh hand seemed at work upon the bellows ;
Old Æolus his fury seemed to vent
  On transport steamers, evidently jealous ;
Blowing sea horses right on board the screw,
And drenching to the skin the working crew.

XXIII

The long night through we spent in grins and groans,
  To stand, or sit, or lie abunk, unable ;
Precautions taking to insure our bones
  Against the risk of lurching chair or table ;
Blasting the fury of the Tyrrhene sea,
And its malignity right fervently.

XXIV

When morning dawned, the weather was no better,
   The good ship often rolling gunwale under;
The mainsail split, whilst a brown fleecy setter,
   Affrighted howled at frequent peals of thunder;
The rain still falling as it meant to swamp us,
And in our movements and our limbs to cramp us.

XXV

And sooth to say the cattle in the hold
   Were found all sea sick! some at point of death;
Shivering and foaming at the mouth, and cold,
   Their lives remaining known but by their breath.
About a score of them were heaved on deck,
At risk of broken limbs, or broken neck.

XXVI

And there they lay, secured upon a tether,
   Now hard a starboard, hard a port back-sliding,
Excoriated all, and doubtful whether,
   They'ld live or die, receiving such a hiding,
When through a rift amidst the raging storm,
We hailed with joy the mountains of Panorme.

XXVII

Favoured by heaven in site, and clime, and soil,
   A heritage of wealth, Trinacria, 's thine!
With no great stretch of industry and toil,
   A harvest, rich in corn, and oil, and wine,
Might make thy barns and cellars overflow;
Thy coldest heart with gratitude to glow.

XXVIII

The gods of ancient Greece, when in the flesh,
  Spent many a happy day upon thy isle ;
And now and then, their memories to refresh,
  Descended from the skies in humble style.
And on pretence of having change of air,
Had rare flirtations with thy winsome fair.

XXIX

Now penury is seen on every hand !
  Beggars in crowds the traveller assail ;
Brigands in gangs still desecrate the land,
  Armed men keep watch upon each royal mail.
Armed to the markets ride thy husbandmen,
And thank their saints when safe at home again.

XXX

Of ancient Grecian type, thy population
  In physique and in form are of the best ;
Forward in bearing—backward as a nation,
  Proud of their vocal cords—given to a jest,
Swarthy as Spaniards, or as Portuguese ;
As fond of holidays, of sloth, and ease !

XXXI

The homesteads of thy peasants are mere sheds,
  The floors of mud, and sometimes even of mire ;
A truss of straw on planks their best of beds ;
  For cooking only each small kitchen-fire.
And, shame to say, hair hunting may be seen
On every door-step, every village green.

XXXII

No forests on your marble mountains grow,
    You cut them all for fuel in your need.
Few streamlets from their arid bosoms flow,
    And scanty are thy wells on dale or mead.
Improvident of timber, you now pay
The penalty in sterile hardened clay.

XXXIII

This is the twenty-first day of December,
    Yet oranges are ripening on the trees ;
The almond is in blossom, that remember !
    The young wheat waves beneath the fresh sea breeze.
Here even the bees toil all the winter through,—
And, what we well could spare, mosquitoes too.

XXXIV

Thy mountains, though so bleak, and bare, and rough,
    Are rich in marbles, beyond all assumption ;
So marmorize the world, they're quite enough,
    And leave enough for thine own home consumption.
Thy valleys, filled with oranges and limes,
Are but the orchards of our northern climes !

XXXV

Greece, Carthage, Rome, the Turks, the Goths, the
    Gauls,
    Have in their turn invaded thy fair land,
And held dominion in thy vaulted halls,
    But left their empire's bones upon thy strand,
For future archæologists to scan,
And prove that race is mortal as mere man !

XXXVI

Palermo ! erst Trinacria's greatest glory,
  Most glorious still you stand upon your bay !
Replete with great events in ancient story,
  As are thy tideways with the finny prey,
Before our Anno Domini was known,
When Carthage ruled the world she called her own.

XXXVII

Protected by thy patron saint, Rosalia,
  Whose bones lie mouldering in their silver urn,
You've got a panacea, *inter alia*,
  For famine, plague, and pestilence, in turn.
You've but to carry round her musty bones,
When, presto ! all is well ! and save your moans.

XXXVIII

So yearly in procession you her ossary,
  With grand devotion, carry through your high street.
To understand which, would require a glossary,
  And make one's understanding *it* a high feat.
Well you remember how, in days of yore,
  The fatal plague she drove from door to door.

XXXIX

In her processions all grades of society,
  Clergymen, laymen, ploughmen, men-of-war,
Doctors and barristers in vast variety,
  All put their shoulders to Rosalia's car.
The car of Juggernaut was but a toy,
Compared to Rosa's car, Palermo's joy.

XL

On Pellegrino we have seen her shrines,
  Some thirteen hundred feet above the sea,
Where pilgrims by the score, drawn up in lines,
  Once in her cavern knelt on bended knee.
Now, there all's desolate !   Her prestige gone !
All's silent ! save the droppings on the stone !

XLI

The saints in Sicily have had their day,
  Their altars stand neglected everywhere.
The passers-by no solemn *Salve* ! pay
  Before their images with pious care,
Though promised forty days of full indulgence
For every *Salve* by the Pope's effulgence.

XLII

There too the Jesuits have had their day,
  And left their country for their country's good
In one grand exodus, in dire dismay :
  Warned by the people in revengeful mood.
Leaving square furlongs of monastic buildings,
With all their statues, paintings, carvings, gildings,

XLIII

Escheated to the State ; perplexed to know
  What use to make of so much vacant space,
For thirty thousand souls, or high or low;
  Enough for every one to find a place.
Why stand they empty whilst thy homeless poor
In beggary and rags besiege each door ?

XLIV

And whither have they fled, both stock and scion?
Both monks and nuns in all their strength of numbers?
To Albion ! where they beard the British Lion,
And mesmerise him as he soundly slumbers :
Unconscious of the toils they knit around him,
Resolved to draw his teeth, and then impound him !

XLV

There thy Sicilians, centuries ago,
For vespers gathered, held their Easter Feast,
And dealt their first avenging bloody blow.
Under the benediction of their priest.
And rose in massacre throughout the isle,
Slaying each trampling Gaul, and caitiff vile.

XLVI

Both day and night the holocaust went on,
And lest some friends should suffer in the strife,
The password *ciccre* was thought upon,
Which Monsieur can't pronounce to save his life.
Thus safely in the dark they hewed them down,
And cut Trinacria free from Anjou's crown.

XLVII.

There thy Toledo stretches from thy bay
For two long measured miles, dry as a bone,
Straight as an alpenstock, smooth as a *dais*,
Clean as the cats had licked it, every stone :
Where even a spider would not be forgiven,
But would be whisked into a cart unshriven.

XLVIII

Within that little tower above the gateway,
  Triumphant, Garibaldi had his home.
And hoisting his dictator's ensign, straightway
  Unto his councils bade thy best men come.
And organised his glorious revolution,
Giving Palermo its new constitution.

XLIX

Thy churches are superlatively fine,
  Their priests more numerous than their congregations.
But there is no devotion in their line,
  All's pantomime or noisy incantations.
The service done by contract, badly done,
Even from the rising to the setting sun.

L

Female confession here seems most to please ;
  What sinners must the pretty creatures be !
We've seen at once a dozen on their knees,
  A dozen clergy listening eagerly,
In no way shocked at all their sins confest,
And their endeavours to make a clean breast.

LI

Indulgences are still sold in the market,
  For forty days at once you may run riot ;
Yea, all the ten commandments you may bark at,
  And keep the beadles and the priesthood quiet
By Aves said at street and roadside altars,   [halters.
Even though your crimes deserved the hangman's

LII

A monast'ry you'll find in every street,
    Large as a barrack for two thousand men,
Some inmates well-shod, some with naked feet ;
    Some only fit to live in hermit's den.
No wonder that the population's poor,
When such excisemen get within the door.

LIII

The everlasting clanging of their bells
    Is grating to the ear beyond endurance.
A public nuisance ! which distinctly tells
    The vast amount of clerical assurance.
What right have they to rob us of our sleep,
And drive us frantic by the bells they keep?

LIV

There's *Ponte Ammiraglio* high and dry,
    Deserted by the stream it once protected :
Stalwart and strong in hoar integrity,
    Just like an injured husband when rejected,
And there his slippery spouse, half dead and dull,
Has got another bridge ; the dirty trull !

LV

And there Marcellus, sallying from Panormus,
    Met Asdrubal advancing in array ;
With a front rank of elephants enormous !
    And drove them scampering into the bay,
Bringing this Punic War unto a close,
And shaking hands with his tremendous foes.

LVI

On Catalfano's crest Jove had his shrine,
  Apollo, Hercules, Minerva—there !
And Isis and Serapis, all divine !
  Had each a temple on that hill-top bare,   .
Whilst far below upon the briny flood,
Revered by sailors, Neptune's temple stood.

LVII

There Carthaginian and Phœnician crews
  Protection claimed from all the ills of the sea,
Paying devoutly every priest his dues,
  And had their prayers allowed obediently.
And Tyrian pirates, far away from shore,
Lowered their flags its blessing to implore.

LVIII

The brick and mortar masonry lies there,
  Bits sunk, bits sinking in the Tyrrhene waves,
The alabaster shafts and marbles rare
  Now ornament Palermo's churches' naves ;
Whilst bits of minor merit thus torn down
Are dovetailed in the walls throughout the town.

LIX

Sirens and Fauns once wantoned on that wold,
  And Pan Pandæan piped his pleasing notes,
And Daphne and Diana both, though cold,
  There had their romps amongst the uncut oats;
There mortal nymphs with demigods were wed,
And of young demigods were brought to bed.

LX

And hence the greatness of the Roman name,
   Their mighty prowess in their mighty wars;
For as all know, each hero known to fame
   Claimed his descent direct from the god Mars,
Palming upon the world, the curtain lie,
Transmitted thence to late posterity.

LXI

But gods and goddesses and god-like men
   Gave way to time; their fanes neglected stood,
Disintegration undermined each den;
   The priesthood died from want of daily food,
A new religion burst upon the world,
And pagan shrines were into ruins hurled!

LXII

Mark well that headland jutting on the sea,
   Those antique ruins once Solunto's glory,
Rough rocks and masonry strewn piteously,
   Once known to fame, now almost lost in story.
Herculean fragments, from their basements hurled,
The veneration of a pagan world!

LXIII

Mark too that upland sloping from the shore,
   Terrace on terrace rising so sublime,
Both broad and wide, and faced with stones of yore,
   That forest dense of olive, orange, lime,
There the Phœnician captains had their home,
The prey of Greece, of Carthage, and of Rome.

LXIV

The Saracens, with fell destructive hand,
  This once Phœnician stronghold tore in pieces,
And Sexton Time with charitable wand
  Entombed its bones beneath thick dusty fleeces,
Till archæologists the other day
Unearthed Solunto from its bed of clay.

LXV

Palermo's magnates, from its first foundation,
  There had their country seats on hill or dale,
And Greek or Saracen, each in his station,
  In Bagaria found a place for sale,
And there they housed their children and their wives,
Returning thence to end their lengthened lives.

LXVI

The very dust of great men strews the sod !
  Whose names shine most in ancient history,
And fertilizes fields where once they trod !
  Their Manes wander under every tree !
Now everything is metamorphosed, save
The sky, the sunshine, and the crystal wave.

LXVII

And Bagaria, once a paradise
  In Saracenic times, is now a ruin !
A populated ruin in disguise !
  Standing yet falling, living, nought renewing !
In cleanliness its tenants scarcely higher
Than are the swine that wallow in its mire.

LXVIII

Its palaces untenanted, neglected stand,
  Their owners bankrupt! reckless absentees!
Their revenues the product of their land,
  Spent far away, perhaps beyond the seas,
And willing hearts, and hands prepared for toil,
From want of labour cumber its rich soil!

LXIX

There stood in ancient grandeur oriental,
  No farther than a mile from the Marina,
Set in its *mare dolce* transcendental,
  The Saracenic Windsor, Al Hacina,
Where Moslem houris welcomed sultans home,
And made a paradise of every dome.

LXX

And there Favara's fountain gently bubbles
  From Mount Grifoni's bosom, pure as ever,
'Midst all the wreck of nations and their troubles,
  Just like a very pretty little river,
Watering the vines and olives as it flows,
A welcome visitor where'er it goes.

LXXI

Of all the dynasties that ruled thy realm,
  The Saracens did *most* for thy prosperity,
None steered thy ship of state with steadier helm,
  No race did so much for remote posterity;
A thousand years have passed away since then,
Yet still the Saracens are model men!

LXXII

Arabia's swarthy sons, whose heads still grace
  The sign-boards of our best of city inns,
With honesty proverbial in their race,
  Their word their bond, their *faith* their worst of sins,
The *bêtes noirs* of Popes and northern tabbies.
With which they wont to frighten naughty babbies,

LXXIII

Those queer old conic towers at every station,
  With water overflowing, trickling down
Like monster stalactites in full formation,
  With subterranean pipes throughout the town,
You owe the Saracens!   Your every spout
Is Saracenic enterprise, no doubt !

LXXIV

Thy Chapel Royal's but a Moslem Musjid
  Of the best style of Saracenic art,
Transformed and re-transformed by most unjust deed,
  Till nothing but the walls remain in part,
The Arabic inscription o'er the door
Is raised : ' No god but God you here adore!'

LXXV

Both Greeks and Normans, Goths and Romans there,
  To our disgust and to their own disgrace,
Of Saracenic grandeur everywhere
  Have done their worst all traces to efface :
Yea, even their groves of palm-trees they cut down,
Of yore the greatest pride of thy old town.

LXXVI

Palermitans ! excuse a word or two
  Upon your everlasting habit, smoking !
The quantity of smoke puffed out by you
  Both morning, noon, and night is most provoking.
The very pavement where you walk or sit
Is wet and grimy with the *gobbs* you spit !

LXXVII

A sharp cross-fire of spittle day and night,
  One must encounter in each public street ;
'Tis really ticklish work to stand upright
  And keep one's patent boots both clean and neat :
No lady dares to walk a dozen paces
Without dire damage to her silks and laces.

LXXVIII

The incense that each smoker yearly offers
  Unto the demon Fashion would, in gold,
Locked up in some Insurance Office coffers,
  Provide a good annuity when old.
It makes men invalids in manhood's prime !
And young men old men long before their time !

LXXIX

So very ardent seems each pallid smoker,
  You'd think that they were paid for by the dozen,
That some tobacconist, become a joker,
  Had used them as a means the town to cozen,
To burn *their* weeds as of the true sublime,
Forking them out a dozen at a time.

LXXX

We've sometimes thought how men would kick and claw
　If ev'ry one that smokes, were forced to smoke
By stern imperative resistless law ;
　They then would think their pastime not a joke,
But plot against the edict as despotic,
And tilt against it with their spears Quixotic.

LXXXI

And now, Palermo, we must say adieu !
　A pleasant sojourn we have had the while;
A future visit we must pay to you,
　Some future winter spend upon thy isle.
'Tis good economy of life at times,
To 'scape the winters of our northern climes !

LXXXII

'Tis no small benison to get away
　From Albion's scathing winds, its snow and sleet,
And sit at open window when we may
　Without a thought of artificial heat,
Courting the sun when we go out to stroll
With *parapluie* for a *parasol !*

LXXXIII

Once more, before they string up the Blue Peter,
　A line or two we pen to thy Marina :
No finer promenade ere stood in metre,
　Search Europe through and you won't find, we ween, a
More noble beach to breathe the balmy breeze on ;
And if you do, we must have lost our reason.

CANTO FIFTH

I

AT last the three days' hurricane is over,
  And bag and baggage we have got on board
The Nomentino steamer, the Sea Rover,
  His hold with railway rolling-stock well stored.
Resolved to make a moderate sort of cruise,
And step ashore in classic Syracuse.

II

A goodly list of passengers he had,
  Both first and second class : some Bersaglieri,
A serjeant's party, in blue tunics clad,
  Tight little fellows, well set up and cheerie,
Besides a score or two of barn-door fowls,
A dog or two, a brace of pet grey owls.

III

We never saw Palermo look so pretty,
  Set in a framework of bright snowy hills,
With orange boxes piled on every jetty,
  And cargo boats with wine casks, and their bills,
The donkey drivers for fresh cargoes galloping,
And with big sticks their donkeys soundly walloping.

IV

Steamers of every nation seaward veering,
  Like swans let loose from a too long confinement;
East, north, and west, each vessel homeward steering,
  Each craft according to its own consignment,
Whilst the Sea Rover stood along the shore;
A royal mail for Trapani he bore.

V

Bright beams the sun on Pellegrino's cliffs,
  Wrinkled by age, and pitted o'er with cells,
Light dance the fishermens' industrious skiffs,
  Lost to the eye at times, between the swells;
Whilst St. Rosalia's ruined shrine looks down,
And on neglectful man appears to frown.

VI

The sea, unruffled as a land-locked bay,
  Had yet a rolling swell, like hills and dales,
Which broke upon the shore in lofty spray,
  Proving the prevalence of recent gales,
Just like a matron after a hot quarrel,
Whose bosom heaves beneath her silk apparel.

VII

St. Vito's Cape now passed, we meet the gale,
  With a head-pitching, heavy-crested sea;
Whilst on the starboard bow we spy a sail
  Right roughly handled—in extremity!
The main and mizen masts gone by the board,
A tattered foresail all she could afford.

VIII

Now in the bay of Trapani we ride,
  All snug, although a storm is outside raging
On the Ægean Sea; the foaming tide
  A ceaseless war against the long reefs waging,
Driving all mariners into the port,
To seek for shelter as a last resort.

IX

Here Rome and Carthage fought for sheer existence,
  In lines tremendous, full five hundred sail,
And Fortune threw her sword, with blind persistence,
  Now in the one, now in the other scale,
Each beaten party rallying from the blow,
Resolved to strike again a deadlier blow.

X

Pius Æneas and his blue-eyed boy,
  With his surviving warriors by his side,
All homeless flying from the siege of Troy,
  Sought refuge here, and rest from wind and tide.
There pitched his camp and made himself at home,
And held his games, ere steering on to Rome.

XI

Behold with wond'rous gaze Mount Eryx rise,
  Where stood the fane of Venus Erycina,
Built by Æneas, goddess-born ! the wise !
  In honour of his mother, La Divina !
Where, with a thousand damsels in her train,
The goddess incense sought, nor sought in vain

XII

Her devotees she counted by the million,
  Of all religions and of every clime,
Each year amassing gold to stuff a pillion,
  Her worship being deemed *the* most sublime,
And there she built her city so amazing,
The old Phœnician *nameless* houses razing.

XIII

Long the stronghold of swarthy Carthaginians,
  Before our Anno Domini was born,
They fought and lost with Romans and Athenians,
  Until at last they found their hopes forlorn,
And yielding to their hard fate left Europa
Finding in Carthage quite sufficient *scopa.*

XIV

Sacked, burnt, destroyed, rebuilt, torn down anew,
  Its ruins scraped together, reconstructed,
A motely mass of masonry you view,
  And Trapăni still standing—ill conducted !
Its people a *melange* of old Illyrian,
Greek, Trojan, Roman, Saracen, and Syrian !

XV

Meum and *tuum* they can't understand;
  Each man's a brigand when he finds impunity;
Ready to risk his life, on sea or land,
  To profit by an easy opportunity.
The courts of Trapani have much to do,
To keep in order such a brigand crew.

XVI

What shoals of fishes still frequent the bay !
　What monsters of the mighty deep, afloat !
Of ev'ry shape and size, its finny prey ;
　Miraculous the draughts of every boat !
A pound a penny is the average price
For whitings and for sardines all so nice.

XVII

What are those tents, you say, so thickly set,
　Fit for a host of thrice ten thousand men ?
Sure their encampment must be rather wet,
　Not one dry square mile in the other ten !
These seeming tents are mounds of salt in store,
Made by the sunshine on the flat sea-shore.

XVIII

Enough to season for a year or two
　The flesh-pots of all Europe, and each roast ;
Right busy is each foreign craft and crew,
　Filling each hold, in bulk, from baskets tossed,
Or to the Euxine or the Baltic bound,
To England, Greenland, or King George's Sound.

XIX

Hard hearted wind and rain ! when will ye cease
　To blow and batter with infernal fury ?
Each day and night the storm seems to increase,
　Nor fish nor fisherman can long endure ye,
Whilst outside on the rocks a ship is stranded,
And, lucky fellows ! all the crew have landed.

H

XX

Eight days and nights with little intermission,
  Both wind and rain have done their worst to harm us;
Each fisherman's in pitiful condition,
  We want a fire both to dry and warm us ;
The town peninsular is quite an island,
And cargo-boats the isthmus cross to dry land.

XXI

Now on the rude Ægean all is still,
  The storm-tossed clouds have settled down to rest,
The antique fishing-boats can scarcely fill
  Their large lateen sails with the wind at west ;
And ply their oars, and stand away each yawl,
Right well prepared with basket, hook, and trawl.

XXII

Clank goes the windlass on each laden craft,
  And cheerly round the capstan run the crew,
Loose hang the topsails ready fore and aft,
  And proudly wave the ensigns, old and new;
Their very dogs appear in great concern,
And jump about, and bark on stem and stern.

XXIII

Once more the good 'Sea Rover's' steam is up,
  And panting for the voyage, whistles loud,
Whilst parting friends have had their coffee-cup,
  And on the shore have mingled with the crowd.
Now we are off into the sea Ægean,
The home-bound sailors singing many a pæan.

XXIV

Home of the Saracen ! in days long past !
Marsala ! God's Own Harbour, known in story,
What mighty nations, bending to the blast,
Have sunk beneath thy waves, embalmed in glory?
Where Cross and Crescent fought for life or death,
And 'No surrender!' screamed with their last breath.

XXV

Here Carthage, Greece, and Rome, all in their prime,
With countless hosts contending, lost and won.
Here Rome put forth her strength, in course of time,
And steered her grand Armada for Cape Bon,
And landing her battalions on the strand,
Besieged great Carthage both by sea and land.

XXVI

There Scipio dealt out his mortal blow,
And Carthage, old in prowess and ill doings,
Of ancient Rome hereditary foe !
Was battered down, and buried in its ruins,
The fleet returning, having on each flag
Deleta est Carthago! as a brag !

XXVII

The world have said the deed was nobly done,
The retribution worthy of the race ;
More bloody monsters never saw the sun,
Destruction, slaughter, slavery their chase !
The savage wild beasts spare each other's lives,
But Carthaginians lived but for their knives.

XXVIII

Here Garibaldi with his thousand men
  Made his descent, and found a welcome ready,
And in Calatafimi made his den,
  And fought and won his first pitched battle. Steady !
On to Palermo next his march directing,
And his grand junction with its force effecting.

XXIX

Now all is peace and quiet in Marsala !
  Nought stirring there but hogsheads of good wine.
The Moor and Saracen ! those sons of Allah,
  O'er their fallen fortunes ceasing to repine,
With merchantmen instead of men of war,
Loading wine cargoes, without fuss or jar.

XXX

Birthplace of Bacchus and his Bacchanalians,
  Who taught you how to grow good wine and drink it,
His craft recording in most choice Idalians.
  Good wine you still grow, all the world think it ;
Your grapes as large as any miller's thumb,
Large as a cherry or a damson plum.

XXXI

Like oranges and limes, the vine is found,
  In vast variety, all grown in line,
According to the aspect of the ground,
  Distinct in tint and taste, and sort of wine,
Trained to light tripod work of slender reeds,
Which firmly bound together meets its needs.

XXXII

Once more the ' Rover' ploughs his watery way,
  Along the surf-fringed shores of this rude sea,
By Pontine Marshes and by headlands grey,
  By Selinuntum's temples on our lee,
Long prostrate in the dust ! An earthquake's spoil,
A mockery of human art and toil !

XXXIII

Cape Marco passed, there rose from the horizon,
  A heavy bank of clouds on starboard bow,
Which the good captain seemed to fix his eyes on,
  And say as much as—We shall catch it now ;
And true, ere old Girgenti was abeam,
The thunder rolled and lightning 'gan to gleam.

XXXIV

Soon a sou'wester blew a perfect gale,
  A leeshore's not a pleasant place at sea,
So shirking Acragas and furling sail,
  The bold ' Sea Rover' bore off gallantly,
Making at one long stretch a prudent offing,
Some passengers protesting, and some scoffing.

XXXV

Behold Girgenti's ruins through the cloud,
  Now almost lost amidst wild rocks and stones,
Its palaces and temples once so proud,
  With grandeur wonderful in their dry bones ;
Eight hundred thousand souls once harboured there,
Where nought is seen but shattered ruins bare.

XXXVI

Where the lone stranger acts a stealthy part,
  Of thieves and brigands in a sort of fear,
His admiration for such works of art
  Allayed by dread of brigands lurking near,
Armed to the teeth with pistol and with knife,
Prepared to have his money or his life.

XXXVII

Our captain proved himself an able seaman,
  And made all snug to meet the coming storm,
(He served his prenticeship upon Lake Leman,
  And captain's papers got in old Panorme);
Arrayed in Mackintosh from top to toe,
He bade defiance to the sailor's foe.

XXXVIII

No harbour for the ' Rover ' in such weather !
  So sou'-sou'-east he gave the ship her course,
The topmasts struck, the boats made fast together,
  Each hatch and skylight battened down with force,
And turning sharply round upon his heel,
He sent a third hand aft unto the wheel.

XXXIX

A roaring hurricane, a storm right hearty,
  Heaved up the seas and breakers mountains high ;
Some dashed on deck just like a boarding party,
  And not a plank from stem to stern was dry ;
Most passengers their berths below attained,
And one sole veteran alone remained.

XL

All terra firma then was lost to view,
   The sea and sky were blended in each other,
Whilst now and then a hungry bold sea mew
   Picked up some stray crumbs in the mighty pother,
So pitching, plunging, reeling, rolling free,
The ' Rover' steamed through all the ills of sea.

XLI

To chronicle the scenes of that dread night
   Would not, we fear, be either kind or civil ;
And ev'ry messmate with his utmost might,
   Would certainly consign us to the devil ;
Suffice to say, when morning dawned so red,
Each passenger was found alive—in bed !

XLII

Mark well that single-masted rolling craft,
   Her huge lateen sail lowered half-mast high,
Scarce higher in the water than a raft,
   Her hull at times quite sunk below the eye,
Scudding before the gale, outstripping all
The crested seas that chase her through the squall.

XLIII

In such a ship as that, St. Paul of yore,
   When bound from Sidon unto Syracuse,
In such a storm, was wrecked on such a shore,
   Saving the lives of all, even all the crews,
Whilst the good ship became a total wreck,
With scarce three planks remaining of her deck.

XLIV

No wonder poor Ulysses lost his reckoning,
   And almost lost his life in the Ægean,
And listened to Calypso to him beckoning,
   Affrighted at sea-monsters so Protæan,
And sought asylum in her friendly isle,
Home-sick and sea-sick, sorrow to beguile.

XLV

At half-past eight we sighted Punto Paulo,
   Most southern promontory of the isle,
And though the sun shone dimly through a halo,
   The drifting rain and sleet had ceased awhile,
But the wind blew in gusts as hard as ever,
And pooping waves rushed onwards like a river.

XLVI

An order given the foresail to let fall,
   These galloping sea horses to outstrip,
Was scarce obeyed, when with increasing squall,
   A mighty breaker burst on board the ship,
Upsetting everything behind the mast,
And making even the captain look aghast.

XLVII

Oh, such a scene we've never seen at sea!
   Soldiers and sailors rolling in the brine,
And cocks and hens all screeching piteously;
   Boxes of oranges, and casks of wine,
Knapsacks and shakos, tin pans and a drum;
Afloat, we're sure, was never seen such scum.

XLVIII

Before another breaker got on board,
  The foresail hauled all taut, began to take,
And the 'Sea Rover' through the azure snored,
  Leaving the foaming billows in his wake;
At noon we rounded-to, off Syracuse,
And so here ends this stormy sort of cruise.

XLIX

On that bare boundless waste of limestone rock,
  Crannied by time, and destitute of soil,
Where the gaunt goatherd tends his hungry flock,
  And husbandry itself in vain would toil,
Without a stone or brick to mark its walls,
Once stood proud Syracusa's marble halls.

L

And yet, as if humanity to mock,
  The tombs and catacombs of earliest days,
Chiselled and tunnelled in the solid rock,
  Still perfect stand beneath the wond'ring gaze,—
No bone, nor dust, nor cenotaph survives,
Nor single record of the best of lives.

LI

In long past times her Tyrants' tombs were lost,
  Even Archimèdes' ashes were bestrewn;
And where's Timoleon's or Hiero's dust
  Is all conjecture, and, in fact, unknown;
Yea, even the grave of the seven thousand Greeks
Remains in doubt, as he will find who seeks.

LII

Yet in that self-same rock, the fish of yore
   Have found a peaceful and a lasting grave,
Close packed as pebbles on a pebbly shore,
   Their shells are sharp as when the pristine wave
Washed them to land some million years ago,
And tombed them in the sand, as you well know.

LIII

There Dionysio's Ear, large as a dome,
   Stands open, ready to transmit a groan ;
The theatres of ancient Greece and Rome
   Are standing still, cut out of solid stone,
With all their spacious corridors complete,
Their every portico, and every seat.

LIV

And there the giant cactus takes its station,
   And sentinels the archways to and fro,—
Most self-supporting plant in all creation,
   For neither earth nor water does it know !
And yet its mighty leaves are moist and rank,
As if it grew in a freshwater-tank.

LV

There's not a church in all Ortygia's town
   Without some plundered marbles in the pile,
The temples of its gods were all torn down
   For building purposes upon the isle,
And pediments and cornices of marbles rare
Are broken down the pavement to repair.

LVI

Even the Cathedral stands on the same floor
  Where once Minerva's sacred temple stood,
Its Doric columns splintered, cracked, and hoar,
  Vamped up with masonry, both rough and rude ;—
Yea, its baptismal font is pagan stone,
But from what temple filched is known to none.

LVII

There, in that area, far below the street,
  The ruins of Diana's temple frown ;
Some twenty columns standing on their feet,
  Reduced to stumps, mere blocks of marble brown !
Yet Ephesus could nothing finer raise
Than that sunk temple in its palmy days.

LVIII

Of Doric Syracuse, the Great Defender,
  The Virgin Goddess here was most adored ;
Minerva dwindled to a mere pretender,
  With whom the most devout could not be bored ;
And every excellence embraced by art
In Dian's temple had a graceful part.

LIX

Her marble statue stood in wond'rous beauty
  Behind her altar, girt with chains of gold
Inlaid with precious stones (all free from duty),
  And draped with tinsell'd garments, fold on fold ;
The saints at Saragossa or Lorette
Could not surpass in richness her toilette !

LX

And early in the morn one might have spied
   Fair damsels tripping to her marble shrine,
Their raven tresses with white fillets tied,
   Each with some living victim in her line,
A kid, a leveret, or pair of doves,
Or other game-bird that Diana loves.

LXI

And kneeling at her altar, on their shins,
   They prayed for intercession with some lover,
Or asked forgiveness for some secret sins,
   Or helping hand, some lost heart to recover,—
And though some think the action rather odd,
The story goes, she has been *seen to nod!*

LXII

This chastest specimen of antique Doric,
   Plundered by pagan Romans and Rome's saints,
Shattered by storms and earthquakes (all historic),
   Buried in rubbish, lost to mortal plaints,
Was built upon as if the ground were plunder,
So that its finding was a sort of wonder.

LXIII

Then archæologists, with pick and shovel,
   And sturdy navvies set to work all hot,
And pulling down each superseding hovel,
   And excavating deeply on the spot,
Disclosed the remnants now exposed to view,
And to the ruins gave importance new.

LXIV

Here gods and goddesses have all been sold,
  Like slaves, to highest bidders, long ago ;
And bits unsaleable and very old
  Were burnt for lime, or stuck up for a show—
As fine a Venus as we've set our eyes on
Was lately found deep sunk in mud ! a prize one !

LXV

Here Arethusa's fountain gurgles still,
  Just on the margin of Ortygia's isle ;
Here Nelson's fleet fresh water had their fill,
  To last them through the battle of the Nile ;
And here St. Paulo, without boots or shoes,
Preached to the town of pagan Syracuse.

LXVI

Whence comes the water of this sacred fountain ?
  How got fresh water here, beneath the sea ?—
No doubt from some far distant, unknown mountain,
  By subterranean passage ever free,—
But Greek mythology stepped in and solved
The Arethusa problem here involved.

LXVII

The Greeks were great in all they put their hands to,
  In carving statues, and in carving lies,
Great in the camp, and even as man to man too,
  Supremely great, and fit to sacrifice
Their lives for love, for honour, or for fame,
Preferring sudden death to lengthened shame.

LXVIII

Let's mount that turret, and from it survey
　　The *carte-de-pays* of this wond'rous scene,
The spacious harbour like an inland bay,
　　With briny ripples spreading so serene,
And narrow inlet, where on either hand,
Plemmyrium and Murciano stand.

LXIX

There the Athenian invading fleet
　　At anchor lay, or hauled their ships on shore ;
There pitched their tents and made their host complete,
　　And Syracusa's downfall sternly swore !—
That host which in retreat was there decoyed,
That fleet which brave Gylippus there destroyed.

LXX

There stands the quarry where the Greeks were penned,
　　Like cattle in a fair, and where the dead
And living were promiscuously denned,
　　And where at lest they had but one death-bed,
Now made a rope-work, where the hussies boil
Their dust for salt, and sell the Attic spoil.

LXXI

These two tall columns standing in the corn,
　　With just rotundity enough to prove
Their Doric origin and fate forlorn,
　　Once graced the temple of Olympic Jove,
Where the Athenians offered rites divine,
And sacrifices heaped upon his shrine.

LXXII

And there Hamilcar pitched his Punic camp,
    Planning the ruin of old Syracuse,
Securely stationed—on each flank a swamp—
    When bold Agathocles, with potter's thews
Attacked them in the dark, and made them run,
And captured every Punic mother's son.

LXXIII

There Anapo, unchanged, through waving weeds
    Steals slow and silent gently to the tide,
'Mongst mallows rank, and tall papyrus reeds,
    And bean-fields redolent, both long and wide,
And sugar-canes, and pumpkins, maize, and vetches,
And lizards, frogs, and snakes—the poisonous wretches.

LXXIV

And there Marcellus, with his Roman skiffs,
    And Roman legions, trained like dogs of war,
Dropped anchor under Achradina's cliffs,
    And tried to force his way through bolt and bar,
And sack the town and carry off the plunder,
To grace his triumph and excite Rome's wonder.

LXXV

When Archimedes, with his engineering,
    His rams and catapults, and rocky masses,
His boiling pitch and lead, and valiant spearing,
    His red-hot sand, and iron, and burning-glasses,
Contrived to make the anchorage too hot,
And foiled each ambuscade and marred each plot.

LXXVI

And once again Marcellus, in disgrace,
   Landed his warlike host upon that plain,
Those ruthless butchers of the human race !
   Who took a pride in their amount of plain.   [walls,
And stemmed that steep, and breached and scaled the
And forced the gates of Syracusa's halls.

LXXVII

No quarter for the vanquished in the city !
   Each citizen was put to death apace !
The young made slaves, the women without pity
   Were forced their haughty victor's tents to grace !
The city razed even to the humblest home !
The plunder carried straightway unto Rome !

LXXVIII

And there Marcellus in triumphal car,
   With all his plunder and his spoils before him,
Apeing the prestige of a god of war,
   Midst multitudes all striving to adore him.
Drove in grand state to pay the gods their dues,
And thank them for the sack of Syracuse !

LXXIX

No monster's so devout as the old Roman !
   Those savages who strewed the earth with ruin !
Making each wealthy potentate their foeman,
   Sieging and sacking, raping and undoing ;
As wolves, though gorged with blood and butcher-meat,
Throttle the flock they have not power to eat.

LXXX

Destruction was a part of Roman nature ;
  They seemed but beasts of prey, and preyed on men.
The cannibals, secure in strength and stature,
  Killed but to live, and victual their vile den.
But ancient Romans killed from dire revenge,
And slaughtered hecatombs for nought but change.

LXXXI

Benighted modern Syracusans !   When
  Will you assert your right to take your place
In the great march of intellect, with men
  Worthy of Italy's regenerate race ?
Shake off your indolence ! strip to the buff !
And show you still inherit Grecian stuff !

LXXXII

Adieu ye drones of modern Syracuse !
  Our route lies northwards over to Lentini ;
So we must change the subject of our Muse,
  And join the astronomic Pellegrini.
To-morrow is the day of the Eclipse,
When o'er the sun's disc Luna slowly slips.

LXXXIII

Still is Ortygia !   The morning bland !
  The road cut deep into the solid stone ;
Where antique graves are seen on either hand,
  And open-mouthed proclaim themselves undone.
There stood Epipolæ in days of yore !
There stands Euryalus, still to the fore !

I

LXXXIV

The Scala Greca we are now descending,
    By easy gradients, smooth as asphalt.
And there Marcellus, further sieging pending,
    Wintered his forces for his fresh assault.
And there Santa Helena, with Santa Croce,
Proclaimed her finding it, by *viva voce*.

LXXXV

That Cross which lay three hundred years in dust
    Beneath the rubbish of the Holy City ;
Proof against moth and worm, dry rot and rust,
    Protected by some intervening pity ;
When all around it crumbled to decay,
And to the laws of nature fell a prey.

LXXXVI

There stands Augusta, famous for the slaughter
    By Anjou's myrmidons so fierce and fell ;
Who butchered every son and every daughter,
    As mediæval history can tell :
Simply for holding out 'gainst Anjou's sway,
And being independent in their way.

LXXXVII

And there Magnisi stands with maze so funny,
    Of stoutest cordage cunningly devised,
In which those grand colossal fish, the thunny,
    (A staple article of food so prized),
Are coaxed from cell to cell until too late
They learn how fatal is their common fate.

LXXXVIII

Now that we've up to Carlentini passed,
    Let's retrospective look, and thence survey
The wondrous hills and dales, and caverns vast,
    We lately witnessed on our weary way ;
The playthings of old subterranean fire,
Which so much dread even to this day inspire.

LXXXIX

There live volcanoes threw up red-hot cinders,
    Large as one's head, large as one's house or hearth,
Which falling to the ground, then broke in flinders,
    And formed the stony crust of mot'er earth,
Whilst showers of ashes quite eclipsed the sun,
And formed those beds of solid tufa stone.

XC

Oh what a grand display of pyrotechnics !
    Compared with which the Prussian cannonading,
With all their Krupp's transcendent gyrotechnics,
    Was but a sort of German gasconading.
Mere schoolboy batteries of toys, with pops,
But fit to frighten daws from chimney tops.

XCI

Lentini, though but now a third-rate town,
    Yet you are famed for ancient pedigree ;
Before the Siculi had settled down,
    Or to the proud Corinthian bent the knee ;
Your Laestroyons, those cannibals of yore,
Picked clean their neighbours' bones and drank their
    gore.

XCII

Then Ceres, in compassion for the brutes,
  Taught them to plough and sow, and reap, and mill,
And of good husbandry to reap the fruits,
  And spirits from the palm-tree to distil.
Pity she could not once again descend,
And teach thy husbandmen their ways to mend.

XCIII

Lentini, I would gladly pass your Lago,
  As a great nuisance and to be eschewed !
With all its fish and fowl, and marsh farrago,
  Its fever-beds and pumpkin-beds so crude,
But that it gives occasion in a trice,
To tender you a bit of good advice.

XCIV

Next time Mount Etna goes into the straw,
  Just have its bantlings shot into thy lake,
Until it's filled without a single flaw ;
  And burn up every fever-hatching brake.
Thy population then will sleep at ease,
Secure from all malarial disease.

XCV

And there stands Etna like a morning bride,
  In glorious effulgence, capped with snow,
With old Catania smoking on its side,
  And Naxos' promontory sunk and low ;
And further on, Mount Taurus and Tormina,
And further still the mountains o'er Messina.

XCVI

Poussin or Claude, or even Salvator Rosa,
  Could find no subject worthier of their art,
No landscape fitter to delight a sposa,
  Or to entangle a fair virgin's heart.
But let us now descend unto Lentini,
And see what's doing by the Pellegrini !

XCVII

There stood assembled in one constellation,
  The dons of starry science, so sublime ;
Each with his satellites, in due gradation,
  And telescopes the finest of the time,
Outseeing far the tools of Galileo,
Copernicus, or Egypt's Ptolemeo.

XCVIII

Galvanic batteries, aneroids, chronometers,
  Polariscopes and spectroscopes a few,
Sextants, thermometers, and actinometers,
  And photographic lenses one or two,
Were all in store, with each his speciality,
To spy the sun eclipsed to its totality.

XCIX

Whilst shorter-sighted mortals, short of pelf,
  Rested contented with a smoky glass,
Or a binocular, just like myself,
  Or even with standing room upon the grass ;
Impatient, waited for the solar show,
Thinking the sun had never moved so slow.

C

True to a second of the time predicted
  By astronomic seers long long ago,
A segment of the moon was seen depicted
  Upon the sun, and rapidly to grow;
Until its disc had dwindled to a crescent,
When presto! all was dark, and all quiescent.

CI

Now twilight darkness spread o'er mead and shore,
  The planets in the heavens began to shine,
All nature seemed absorbed in solemn awe,
  The day seemed struck with premature decline.
The barn-door fowls and pigeons went to bed,
And bats and owls flew screeching overhead.

CII

Another solar crescent soon was cleared,
  As when one sovereign o'er another slips;
The welcome daylight rapidly appeared,
  And soon there was an end of the eclipse,
With brilliant sunshine all the afternoon,
Putting desponding Nature into tune.

CIII

Whether the dons with pantoscopic scan
  Saw more than we did with the naked eye
Remains in doubt, but certainly each man
  Descried the working of a power Most High;
Which keeps in harmony sun, moon, and star,
Without a contact and without a jar.

CANTO SIXTH

I

ALL hail, Mount Etna ! glorious from all time
  With base all tropical, and apex snow,
Puffing pale smoke, like summer clouds sublime,
  With not a cinder or a spark to show
The molten lava heaving in thy breast,
Ready to bubble o'er at thy request.

II

In times long past, when restive in thy mood
  You shook the earth, and set the heavens on fire,
And through Catania rolled thy lava flood,
  And broke down every palace, church, and spire,
Wafting their ruins right into the sea,
And spoiled its harbour in thy phantasy.

III

But now thou'rt wiser grown, and thy hot youth
  Is sobered down.   Thy head is silvered o'er,
And men have learned to trust you, and in sooth
  Have built Catania grander than before,
Using thy lava for their building stone,
Paving its streets and squares with it alone,

IV

In every street a lava quarry's found!
   Lava enough lies lumb'ring up thy tide,
So build a new port, larger, more profound,
   Where ships securely might at anchor ride ;
And from beneath thy lava beds there flow
Abundant fountains, as all sailors know.

V

Though 'mongst the world's most lofty mounts you rank,
   You've raised yourself to such supreme degree,
By ash and lava in rude order banked,
   Stratum on stratum, upwards from the sea,
And like the foremost of our self-made men
You're modest in demeanour and in ken.

VI

What leagues of lava lie around thy cone !
   Deposits of all eras from Time's dawn.
Like mountain torrents, hardened into stone,
   Whilst every here and there young craters yawn,
Ready to carry out thy high command,
And pour their filial streams down to the strand.

VII

Whence came these wondrous floods of molten ore?
   What makes the earth to tremble in its ire?
Geologists have told us in their lore
   Our mother earth is but a globe of fire,
With a hard crust, just like an orange rind,
And that an earthquake's caused by pent-up wind.

VIII

That rumbles in its bowels when confined,
  And jerks hot lava upwards through the crater,
A sort of safety-valve of the same kind,
  In fact, exactly of the self-same nature,
As is the siphon standing by your glass;
Open the valve, out spurts the pent-up mass.

IX

Whence comes that misty cloud upon the mountain,
  Seeming at rest, or fasten'd by a tether?
And whilst it sits there, mortal man can't count on
  A single day of settled pleasing weather.
Look through this telescope, and you will find
The cloud is drifting fast before the wind.

X

Windward condensing, as the moist warm air
  Reaches the mountain-top begirt with snow,
Leeward evanishing and turning rare,
  Like steam escaping in its upward flow.
Subject to nature's atmospheric sway,
The law of reproduction and decay.

XI

Catania owes her very soil to thee,
  Brought forth by throes of labour from thy womb,
With all its rich and rare fertility,
  Food for the living, for the dead a tomb!
Her ev'ry fountain, vineyard, fruit and flower,
Her wines and oranges, her every shower.

XII

Catania ! forgive my want of taste
   In asking what on earth you mean to do
With your monastic institutions waste,
   Your empty monasteries old and new?
You've three and twenty got within thy walls;
A world of masonry that quite appals.

XIII

In this same city these said twenty-three
   Monastic institutions—right snug homes—
Are large as palaces, as you may see,
   With marble porticoes and lofty domes ;
You'd think this earth and all the fulness thereof,
Was made by heaven for monks and nuns to bear off.

XIV

With so much acreage of habitation,
   No doubt you're sadly puzzled what to do,
And how to get the needful population ;
   There's only one alternative in view,
And that's to marry every monk and nun,
And raise new citizens : and why not done?

XV

Thy wealth expended in monastic buildings
   Exceeds all human power of calculation ;
Their precious stones, their carvings and their gildings,
   Are fit for crowned heads of the greatest nation.
And yet their founders gravely preached humility,
And penitence, and penance, and servility !

XVI

For instance—thy St. Nicholas is grand
  As any royal palace anywhere !
Its cost would build a harbour on your strand,
  New pave your city, every public square;
Around Mount Etna make a turnpike road,
Or make a people's park both long and broad.

XVII

Catania ! you're neglecting this fine pile ;
  You're bound to take it under special care.
Make it your future Alma Mater, while
  You house all students and professors there.
Let arts and sciences there find a home !
And out of so much wasting good will come.

XVIII

And whence the source of this monastic wealth
  That drained the life-blood from the very nation ?
The greater part of it was got by stealth !
  From dying men in moribund prostration !
By running up enormous shriving bills,
And getting paid by codicils to wills !

XIX

And yet 'twas not the destitute and poor,
  That were allowed to claim asylum there ;
But high-born reprobates, turned out of door,
  Whom their paternal homes could gladly spare,
And there they rolled in elegance and ease,
With every luxury in life to please.

XX

And when rich benefices vacant fell,
    An abbot's, or a dean's, or bishop's stole,
None trumpeted their sacred claims so well,
    Or had more voters at the Chapter's poll.
Even some such rubbish hoped to be made Pope,
Whose fittest vestment was a hempen rope.

XXI

Oh, God! it makes the heart sick thus to find
    THY WORSHIP prostituted by such knaves!
Who've thus contrived to have themselves enshrined,
    And knelt to by weak women and male slaves,
Beside THY ALTAR and on bended knee,
As if such creatures deities could be.

XXII

Thy priests assess you in your very cradle,
    And every year you live, you're sure to drop
Some bits of gold into their wooden ladle;
    Even in the grave this black-mail does not stop,
For, far beyond it, they your heirs will worry
For fees to get you out of purgatory.

XXIII

Perhaps, Italia, there is no occasion
    To twit you thus, and tell you you are loaded
With a huge burden, baneful to the nation;
    And that to kick your loads off you are goaded.
Some years ago your eyes were opened wide,
And on some remedy you'd to decide.

XXIV

Thy legislature, therefore, were so bold
   To put an end to all monastic hoardings,
Life-rented all incumbents, young and old,
   Compounding for their gabardines and boardings,
Annexed such properties unto the State,
Or sold them to the people at low rate.

XXV

And now, Catania, ere we make our *boo*,
   We beg you'll give your people a new park ;
You've cactus-covered lava fields *enew*,
   Which you could turn to this account ; and hark !
Beside your railway station you will find
Acres enough to please the public mind.

XXVI

A jolly railway run we've had to day
   Along the shores of the Ionian Sea,
From Etna's city to Messina's bay,
   Not more than seventy miles, as you may see.
Yet you may wander the whole earth around,
And find no transit with more interest crowned.

XXVII

There, facts and fictions of stupendous weight
   Have had their day, and filled the rolls of fame !
What mighty fleets have sailed into this strait !
   What mighty armies played war's bloody game !
What regions so abounding in fertility !
What marbles rich even where there's most sterility.

XXVIII

There sage Ulysses, with his storm-tossed crew,
  Sought shelter in that little rock-bound bay,
And had with Polypheme an interview,
  Who kindly asked them to prolong their stay;
And like big fools they did so, and were eaten
Ev'ry man Jack!   But U. would not be beaten.

XXIX

The story's much too long for us to tell ;
  There are the rocks that Polyphemus threw !
Hoping they 'ld sink Ulysses down to hell ;
  Just read old Homer, and you'll find it true.
And that's the ' Psyche ' British man of war,
Wrecked on said rocks, all standing every spar.

XXX

The British astronomic deputation,
  Sent out to watch the cause of the eclipse,
Although long-sighted in their own vocation,
  Knew nought whatever of the draught of ships,
Were all on deck, when ' Psyche ' went slap-bang
Upon the rocks till every iron plate rang.

XXXI

Britannia's ships of war seem now too many !
  You 'ld think she felt her fleet a serious evil,
And now and then appoints a perfect Zany,
  To take command, and send one to the *deevil*,
Regardless of the purse of poor John Bull,
Who pays the piper, like an arrant fool !

XXXII

On that low lava point, thick mantled o'er
  With orange, lemon, almond, fig, and vine,
Stood Naxos some two thousand years and more,
  And near it stood divine Apollo's shrine,
And in its bay the Greeks refreshed their crews,
When bent on laying siege to Syracuse.

XXXIII

The bay is still as perfect as of yore,
  The anchorage safe, the sands as soft as ever,
The fish still finest on Trinacria's shore,
  And there from Etna rushed down many a river,
Mere driblets now, with no more water stored,
Than a blackbeetle easily could ford.

XXXIV

And there Hamilcar, marching with long stride
  To be avenged on haughty Syracuse,
Was by the red-hot lava turned aside,
  Which stream he did most shockingly abuse,
Having to march his troops round Etna's cone,
With many an outward curse and inward groan.

XXXV

And there Mount Taurus, beetling o'er the brine,
  Displays its marbles rich, of every shade,
Fit for a convent column, or a shrine,
  An altar railing, or a church façade.
Its marble used to build up towns sublime,
To mend the roadways, or to burn for lime.

XXXVI

See nestled on the cliffs o'er the Marina,
  Old Naxos' daughter, heiress of her fame,
Cursed in her heritage and fate—Taormina !
  The wreck of conquest, both by sword and flame !
Just like a chestnut tree cut to the ground,
That shoots fresh saplings the old stem around.

XXXVII

There Garibaldi with his patriot band,
  Proud of the freedom given to Sicily,
Embarked, and landed them on Reggio's strand,
  And forwards unto Naples stretched the knee,
Driving the worthless Bourbons from their throne,
And laid free Italy's foundation-stone !

XXXVIII

Messina ! favoured both by sea and land,
  You've got as fine a site for thy old city,
As fair a harbour ready to your hand,
  As ere was bought by gold, or won by pity ;
Quite deep enough to drown thy lofty dome,
Or for a shoal of whales to form a home.

XXXIX

Most highly favoured by all northern nations,
  Their greatest pride's by sea to pay you court,
And off thy city to take up their stations,
  Or drop their anchors in thy splendid port ;
And load their ships as full as they can cram
With fruits, and wines, and oil, and corn, and yam.

XL

Soon after preaching to the sage Athenians,
  St. Paolo landed here, and gave *the letter*
The Virgin Mary wrote to the Messinians,
  And which (in order to preserve it better),
The chapter locked in the Duomo's altar ;
And lest the people in their faith should falter,

XLI

A festival was fixed on once a year ;
  And though the first took place in forty-two,
As by church calendar is made most clear,
  Yet at said festa absentees are few ;
In sooth none grander's held in rich Messina,
In honour of *Madonna la Regina!*

XLII

Nothing in ancient or in modern story
  Could show a parallel to her processions !
Even mediæval Rome's ecstatic glory,
  No festa could turn out with such transgressions ;
Rome's virgins, saints, and seraphs, were mere plaster,
At best of marble or of alabaster.

XLIII

But in Messina, idols, all alive,
  Fresh from their mother's arms were therein carried ;
And many a youngster, when disposed to wive,
  There found a virgin, willing to be married ;
And every babe in its respective grade,
Was marked by favour for the part it played.

K

XLIV

Though thy cathedral is but somewhat rude,
  Its granite columns torn from pagan shrines,
Its architecture of a mixture crude,
  More noted for its cubits than fine lines,
Yet its high altar is a perfect gem ;
Of Florentine mosaic, stern to stem.

XLV

You, too, have had your monks and nuns in number
  Surpassing credence, and of every order ;
Black, red, and white, and grey, and blue, and umber,
  Hoarding along thy city's mountain border ;
Why don't you open every padlock'd door,
And comfortable homesteads give thy poor ?

XLVI

As for their wardrobes filled with vestments rich,
  Of silk and satin stuffs, of crape and lace,
With gold and silver stiffened every stitch,
  Fit e'er a bishop or a dean to grace,
Send them to England, where the high-church party
For all such wares now give a welcome hearty.

XLVII

A finer landscape on a Christmas morn
  Than thine is seldom witnessed here below ;
Constantinople's gorgeous Golden Horn,
  'Tis true, surpasses it a shade or so ;
But Europe elsewhere you may search in vain,
And unconvinced take up your place again !

XLVIII

There Aspramonte, Garibaldi's mountain,
  Is wreathed in snow and capped with misty clouds
Feeding in Reggio every city fountain,
  Majestic, towering o'er its vassal crowds.
There his red gilets Garibaldi led;
And there, oh shame! he for his country bled.

XLIX

Strange that Italia's soldiers shot *him* down
  For striving thus to set Italia free!
Sweating to weld anew Italia's crown,
  And make one kingdom of all Italy;
Aiming, though single-handed, to drive home
The sword that lately liberated Rome.

L

Messina, grateful to preserve his name,
  Has after Garibaldi named her high street;
Catania and Palermo did the same,
  And many other cities did a by-street;
But Romans lately in their jubilee
Forgot the Man that taught them to be free!

LI

Messina!—it was only yesterday
  We praised your clime and landscape to the skies,
And those who were not there might almost say
  How fond he is of painting in disguise!
But, female-like, without e'er rhyme or reason,
With wind and rain you've jeopardised your season.

LII

You've lashed yourself into a blasted rage,
    Just like Xantippe, that most arrant shrew,
Laughed even to scorn the weatherwise so sage,
    And emptied pots of water on our screw ;
You've torn your bright blue sky serene to rags,
And dashed your chimney-cans upon the flags.

LIII

But, like good Socrates, our ' Pluto ' casts
    Aside thy deluge, with a sailor's scorn ;
His pennants three now flutter on the masts,
    And right into the Straits the ship is borne ;
A shoal of dolphins join in the convoy,
And of right dirty weather wish all joy.

LIV

Soon Scylla and Charybdis, wreckers both,
    Rivals in trade, scowled fiercely at each other,
Whirling and foaming in their self-made froth,
    Which now no cock-boat puts into a pother ;
No cabin-boy now cares a pinch of snuff
For all old Homer's Odyssean stuff.

LV

Soon as we opened out the Tyrrhene Sea,
    A fierce nor-wester took us on the bow,
Which made the ship lurch heavily a-lee,
    And roll amongst the billows like a sow ;
Whilst every now and then his chaps were doused,
And every griff on deck was soundly soused.

LVI

The gallant ' Pluto' nobly did his duty ;
  Clyde-built, a Clydesman for his engineer,
The crew Sicilian, and a little sooty,
  And right well did the helmsman ' Pluto' steer ;
So all the passengers sat down to dinner,
Right peckishly inclined, both saint and sinner.

LVII

First came anchovies, raw as from the pickle ;
  Then vermicelli soup, with Parma cheese,
Both only meant the appetite to tickle ;
  Then came the fish—the sword-fish, if you please,
Which seem'd to stick in every third man's gizzard,
As done on purpose by some Northern wizard.

LVIII

First three, and then some others left the table,
  As if each nose at once began to bleed,
Then rushed below as fast as they were able,
  And called the steward in their utmost need.
And then there was a rattling of ship's crockery,
At which some old files winked in silent mockery.

LIX

The dark night through, the ' Pluto' pitched and rolled,
  Just like a living creature sadly sea-sick,
Whilst sympathetic groanings manifold   [sick,
  Up through the gratings came, and made even me
Such castings-up of bad accounts, I ween,
On board ship I have neither heard nor seen.

LX

And when the morning dawned, old Capri's isle,
   And Cape Sorrento loomed in fog ahead,
Whilst as proud 'Pluto' dashed in splendid style,
   Vesuvius seemed to rise just out of bed,
A bed of clouds, with a new nightcap on
Of virgin snow, bright with the rising sun !

LXI

'See Naples, and then die,' is somewhere said,
   But in what book of saws we don't remember;
Yet many of our friends were almost dead,
   Before they saw it—last day of December;
It seemed as if the night would never end,
That from their ailings they could never mend.

LXII

The harbour entered, and the anchor dropped,
   The sea-sick patients mingled in the strife,
Most woe-begone ! each by a strong arm propped,
   As if ten years were added to each life;
And as they took their places in the boat,
All firmly vowed no more to go afloat.

LXIII

This is the first day of another year,—
   A day of sunshine, cloudless all, and glorious !
The atmosphere so still, the sky so clear !
   The temperature so genial, so notorious !
The sea, late tempest-tossed, now laid to rest,
Save where the sea-gulls dapple its smooth breast.

LXIV

Vesuvius, asleep beneath its vapour,
  Has not a breeze to blow the cloud away ;
Castellamare shows its masts so taper,
  Sorrento but a long shot cross the bay,
Exchanges glances, far across the tide,
With Posilippo, on the other side !

LXV

Whilst Capri, like an iceberg on the ocean,
  In blue transparency appears to float,
And stately ships, so late perpetual motion,
  Still as the isle stand, hull and jolly-boat,
Whilst all on board partake of jolly cheer,
And pay obeissance to the infant year.

LXVI

All Naples, like a hive of bees at swarming,
  In holiday costume is on the wing,
Their toilets and their tempers all so charming,
  Bent for this day at least to have their fling,
From Baiæ to Pompeii all's one rattle,
Both young and old ones all upon the prattle.

LXVII

The sunshine, doubled by the sun's reflection,
  Gives Napoli a climate most superb,
With vegetation rich and bronze complexion !
  For man and beast in season every herb ;
No clime on earth is more divinely gifted,
And this will hold good, all the more it's sifted.

LXVIII

"Tis hard to see the magnates, great in wealth,
   Immure themselves in sombre shady courts,
So véry reckless of their precious health,
   Live hybernised in most obscene resorts,
When heaven's best blessings, and without alloy,
On Posilippo's crest they might enjoy.

LXIX

O'er Pozzuoli now the sun is setting,
   And what a sunset for a New Year's Day!
Each purple cloud outlined with golden fretting,
   Islands and continents in grand array,
Set in a golden ocean ultra-tropical,
All transubstantial and kaleidoscopical!

LXX

More beautiful the landscapes in the skies
   Than any scenes below them on the earth!
Dissolving views, transformed before our eyes!
   Each mountain, cape, and rock of recent birth,
Fading away and dying, shade by shade,
'Till darkness closed the scene and all unmade.

LXXI

The night is lovely as the day just gone,
   The moonless vault lit up with starry light,
Where stars and planets sparkle, every one
   In rivalry, with rays divinely bright,
Rolling their orbs through universal space
Harmonious all upon their heavenly race!

LXXII

Old Napoli, your city's much too small
 For such a multitude of out-door tartars ;
You greatly want a new one, wherein all
 Thy surplus population can find quarters ;
'Tis truly perilous to walk your streets,
And run the gauntlet through the crowd one meets.

LXXIII

You've got the finest site for a new city
 That all Italia can give, from north to south ;
With such an outlet 'tis a monstrous pity
 Your citizens should live from hand to mouth :
On Posilippo's slopes go build a new one,
For there you'll find *the* site—we think the true one.

LXXIV

For thy great trade you need another port !
 Why don't you tumble down thy Castel d'Ovo,
And make a sea-wall of its bones, in short,
 And have a steamboat harbour all *de novo* ?
Why don't you tunnel through your Piz-Falcone,
And new roads make to thy Chiatamone ?

LXXV

And give a pier to land on at one's ease,
 Secure from boatmen and such sharks and sharpies,
Who pull, and haul, and tug, and tear, and tease,
 And pounce upon the stranger just like harpies,
And make the landing a severe infliction !
A grievance far beyond the power of diction !

LXXVI

What wonderful spectàcle have we here,
  That crowds the thoroughfare and piazzetta!
What means that bravo? that exulting cheer?
  That Accidente? Morte? and Vendetta?
'Pilone's captured! killed in the affray!
And there his body lies on the cold clay!'

LXXVII

PILONE, long the terror of the city,
  The brigand chief, so cruel and so daring,
Who killed or plundered hundreds without pity,
  Or made them captive, no rich subjects sparing,
And put a price upon each precious life,
With threats of pistol-shot, or bloody knife.

LXXVIII

No qualms of conscience in that rugged breast
  Conflicted with the mandate, 'Do not kill.'
He killed but for his bread and to exist,
  And pay his wife and children's weekly bill;
His doomsday-bill acquitted by the Church,
Which no good Catholic leaves in the lurch.

LXXIX

But yesterday, secure in his disguise,
  He stole a march in quest of some black-mail,
When, to his horror and intense surprise,
  Five stout policemen, put upon his trail,
Closed round him, as he sternly stood at bay,
Defiant, desperate, in dread array!

LXXX

Short was the conflict ! bloody the defence !
  Pilone, fighting, fell upon his gore,
Vowing revenge with virulence intense.
  His lifeless corpse they to the station bore,
And there it lies, exciting horror deep,
Calm and quiescent all, as if asleep !

LXXXI

All passion disappears with the last breath,
  Before the mortal spoil is still and cold !
No smoother of the brow like sudden death,
  Which exorcises rage in young and old,
And throws a saint-like smile upon the face,
And o'er each rugged feature form and grace.

LXXXII

We've seen the victim of assassination
  Lie cold and lifeless on his bloody bed,
We've trod the battle-field on grand occasion,
  And scanned the features of the heaps of dead :
No horror, rage, nor agony was seen,
But peace, composure, rest, upon each mien.

LXXXIII

Pilone was devout, observed each festa
  Of the Madonna and his patron saint,
And soundly slept in bed or in *siesta* ;
  These amulets and crosses, rude and quaint,
He worshipped on occasions far from home ;
His Lares and Penates left in Rome !

LXXXIV

Palace, of royal palaces the grandest
    That Italy can boast of, great Caserta !
A vanity of vanities, thou standest,
    With all thy glories, but one great Deserta !
The sentries that protect you, all you shelter,
With all your acreage of tiles and spelter.

LXXXV

A paradise, without an Eve or Adam
    To cull its flowers and banquet on its fruits !
Its footpaths made of pulverised macadam,
    Brisk crystal streamlets wat'ring ev'ry root,
A naked sword, suspended in the air,
Debarring its late owner's entrance there.

LXXXVI

The Bourbon, if he knew not how to rule,
    Was master of the art of palace-building ;
In theatres and ball-rooms not a fool ;
    In sculpture, stucco, fresco, painting, gilding,
No richer combination will you find
Comprised beneath one roof, of ev'ry kind.

LXXXVII

And yet this is but one of many other
    Right royal palaces of Bourbon line,
In which some monarch lived, or monarch's brother,
    Who claimed right thus to live by gift divine ;
Whilst their most humble millions lived in styes,
Story on story built, up to the skies.

LXXXVIII

Let's halt a day at Capua, and view
  The Carthaginian winter camp of yore;
Those cutthroats, to their thirst for conquest true,
  As witnessed in Sicilia before,
Here strong in strength of numbers, art, and science,
Setting Rome's laws and legions at defiance.

LXXXIX

Here Hannibal, victorious from the fight   [down,
  Of Cannæ, pitched his camp and trenched each
And billetted his soldiers as a right.
  Upon the citizens throughout the town,
Who spent the winter in inglorious ease,
Wanting in nothing that their tastes could please.

XC

Whom Roman art of war had failed to quell
  The Roman art of love at length subdued;
The dupes of women s blandishments, they fell
  At last a prey to Roman soldiers rude,
And fertilized the fields where once they lay,
Or toiled in bondage, sorrow, and dismay.

XCI

The last men of that stalwart swarthy race,
  Who darkened the bright shores of Italie,
Inflicting on it much intense disgrace
  And ravaging its goods by land and sea;
No Afric legions daring evermore
To plant a foot upon Europa's shore.

CANTO SEVENTH

I

THE dreary weary night has passed away,
  Though at express-rate we have travelled through,
And gladly do we hail the light of day,
  Tinting with rose the Alban hills so blue,
Paling the morning star and waning moon,
And putting human nature into tune.

II

Velletri! cries the guard. Each sleeping limb,
  Stiff as a crutch, is shampooed into action,
Whilst church-bells call their flocks to matin hymn,
  And cattle-carts creak past in sluggish traction,
Laden with pumpkins, cucumbers, and melons,
Whilst in the van are locked a pair of felons.

III

Brigands ! just captured on Mount Ariano,
  Amidst the Alban mountains long the terror,
Forcing a living there, all so *piano*,
  That Justice often fell into an error ;
Till treachery at last stepped in and told
Their ways and means, and trapped them in their hold.

IV

Partenza ! cries the guard ; the train careers
   Adown the Alban slope with speed alarming.
The morning mist, so dense, soon disappears,
   Unfolding to the gaze bright landscapes charming,
Albano, Monte Cavo, and Frascati,
With here and there a string of stolid *frati.*

V

St. Peter's rears aloft its mighty dome,
   Triumphant over Rome's three hundred shrines,
All scattered broadcast through the streets of Rome,
   In sacred fancy free, by its divines,
Each vieing with its neighbour as to station.
And tower, and spire, and dome, and ostentation.

VI

Now through the wild Campagna we career,
   'Mid shapeless ruins standing on each hill,   [steer
'Mongst which the big-nosed sheep and long-horned
   Graze uncontrolled, and fatten at their will,
Whilst aqueducts in endless ruin run,
Warmed by the radiance of the morning sun.

VII

What have we here ?   The meet ! a hunting party
   Assembled on the knoll in bright array,
With carriage loads of ladies, all so hearty
   In demi-toilet, chatty, witty, gay,
Prepared to mount and mingle in the canter,
Or 'mongst those broken arches have a saunter.

VIII

And there sneaks Reynard, looking out for shelter,
  Trained to the sport, and making for some *earth*,
Right well assured, through all the helter-skelter,
  To reach his hiding-place—his place of birth !
And not a bit affrighted at the fray,
Prepared to run again some other day. .

IX

Now close we with the aqueduct *Felice*,
  The grandest waterwork of the old city,
Fed by the Alban hills ; repaired, *si dice*,
  By Gregory the Sixteenth out of pity ;
Still, as of yore, refreshing many a home
With best spring-water, led through modern Rome.

X

Go, view the fountain Trevi, so abounding,
  Break into its piazza, like a river,
In artificial grandeur so astounding,
  Summer and winter, there cascading ever,
And judge what waterworks Rome could conceive,
And what in solid fact she could achieve.

XI

Now through a breach made in the olden walls
  At slackened pace we roll into the station.
Roma ! at last the *conduttore* calls,
  And soon we clear the wicket in rotation,
And o'er the Esquiline to the Costanza
We jostle on, and there secure a *stanza*.

XII

What ails old Porta Pia's towers of brick,
  Its sculptured gate, tiara, and cross keys,
Its antique walls of masonry so thick,
  Its splintered columns and tall cypress trees ? [them,
Perhaps some earthquake's sudden shock has shattered
Or band of brigands from Soracte battered them.

XIII

Well ! these are shot-holes made by cannonading,
  The massive gate is like a target torn ;
That breach was made for soldiers escalading ; ·
  These trees stood in the way and so got shorn,
The pope's own scutcheon sculptured overhead
Is smashed to fragments, just like gingerbread.

XIV

The guardian marble angels in their niches
  Are cripples made without a leg to stand on,
And the Madonna, whom each priest beseeches,
  On this occasion they had to abandon,
As she stood full length, radiant o'er the keystone,
A mark for shot and shell and bits of freestone.

XV

There Freedom, wearied of continued knocking
  To gain admittance in the way they preach,
With round shot forced an entrance, no doubt shocking,
  And marched her Bersaglieri through the breach
On to the Capitol, their rightful home ;
And Roman bondsmen freemen made of Rome.

L

XVI

Great was the dread of all the Papalini !
   The gaudy Zouaves skedaddled in retreat ;
Intense the joy of all the Cittadini !
   The triumph of the people was complete ;
The tricolore from every window waved ;
The long-lost liberty of Rome was saved.

XVII

And when the troops along the street paraded,
   A thousand thanks each man had to endure.
The victors soon were vanquished, barricaded,
   The buttons on their coats were scarce secure ;
The girls were ripe to fall into their arms,
And plucked their cocktail plumes, to keep as charms.

XVIII

Whence all this pomp, and noise, and frantic gladness,
   This Carnevalian outburst by surprise?
Last year Rome mourned in solemn silent sadness,
   With discontent in man and woman's eyes !
Now o'er each window tricolores are waving,
And men and women masked are rampant raving.

XIX

For ages crushed beneath oppression's rule,
   Their souls and bodies both alike enslaved,
They strove in vain to break each papal tool,
   And join their nation's standard humbly craved,
With Vatican array they could compete,
But from French chassepots they had no retreat.

XX

At last their griefs and groans were heard on high :
  The Gallic legions fierce were ordered home
To prop their despot and his destiny ;
  Then for the Romans Freedom's hour had come :
The Porta Pia's walls were battered down,
And Rome annexed unto Italia's crown.

XXI

Hence all this mirth and masking jubilee,
  These clouds of standards, and these grotesque cars,
The people's joy at thoughts of being free,
  These showers of bon-bons and these wordy wars,
All borne with temper, harmony, and grace,
In due decorum both in serge and lace.

XXII

And where are now the shepherds of the flock,
  With all their dogs, and crooks, and rods, and whacks ?
Who hedged them like a ring fence on a rock,
  And tore the fleeces off their very backs ?
All chased across the Tiber, high and low,
Afraid their faces to their sheep to show.

XXIII

And where is now the Despot so imperious
  (By grace of God and by the people's will),
Who fenced oppression round with force mysterious,
  And trod the Romans down with so much skill,
Who crushed a noble people nobly fighting
For liberty and law and their self-righting ?

XXIV

Torn from his throne and his Imperial power !
 Burst like a frog by overweening pride !
Now in a German prison glad to cower,
 A laughing-stock to all the world wide ;
A victim to his rage for interference !
A sacrifice for all his incoherence !

XXV

Where are his legions and their Chassepot rifles,
 That at Mentana did such bloody wonders ?
Where is De Failly, who ne'er stood on trifles,
 But belched his shot and shell like mimic thunders ?
Disarmed, dishonoured, desolate, unmanned !
All prisoners of war in Vaterland !

XXVI

What means this solemn stillness of the morn ?
 No cab nor car is heard upon the stones !
No bleating milch-goats and no herdsman's horn,
 No newsboys' calls, nor bells in matin tones !
Yet daylight enters through the window sashes,
And down the chimney gleams upon the ashes.

XXVII

Mercy upon us ! Rome is under water !
 Last night the Tiber must have burst its banks ;
The city's got on hand a serious matter ;
 The people float from house to house on planks,
Along the Corso river-boats are sailing,
And women half dressed at the windows wailing.

XXVIII

Old Tiber, choked with rubbish, silt, and ruin
  Is now unequal to this grand occasion,
When snows are melting, drenching rains are brewing,
  With southern winds and spring-tides in rotation,
And hence the pent-up flood is forced to break
Its crumbling banks and any outlet take.

XXIX

Though very lamentable such excesses,
  Old Rome will profit by this inundation ;
Its ill-kept streets and horrible recesses
  Must undergo a rare purification.
And vaults that shocked the stranger as he passed,
Their owners will be forced to *muck* at last.

XXX

What grand mortality 'mongst rats and mice,
  'Mongst centipedes and beetles, newts and lizards,
Spiders and scorpions, bugs, fleas, and lice,
  That could be rooted out by none but wizards.
What hecatombs of parasites untold
Have now been sacrificed in every hold !

XXXI

That bauble take away ! 'tis here illegal,
  Which lately figured o'er that palace gate,
Emblem of power divine, as well as regal,
  Of mystic union both of Church and State,
A superhuman power on earth to prove,
An archangelic power in heaven above.

XXXII

These keys and diadem have had their day;
   The papal rule in Rome is at an end;
For fifteen hundred years it had its sway,
   And now unto the new *régime* must bend;
The people will the baneful tie to sever,
And rule themselves henceforward and for ever.

XXXIII

This palace for a senate-house is wanted;
   A Roman senate soon must sit in Rome!
Rome's ancient prestige as of yore so vaunted
   Must rise again, and from its ashes come:
Regenerate Romans, proud of antique name,
Aspire once more to fill the rolls of fame.

XXXIV

Misruled, enslaved, impoverished, in despair!
   For fifteen hundred years they wept in chains;
In foreign climes their children had to bear
   An exile's lot, and pinch on slender gains,
Whilst their proud city crumbled to decay,
Or piecemeal to some Vandal fell a prey.

XXXV

Her once great glories are but wrecks and ruins,
   Torn down by Popes to build themselves a name;
A family palace, by their direful doings;
   Regardless of the scandal and the shame.
Using each grand old structure as a quarry
Which Pontiff's power gave them a right to harry.

XXXVI

And recent popes who stopped the barb'rous plunder,
　　And propped with brickwork, arch and architrave,
The columns and pilasters rent asunder,
　　And rescued them from a too early grave.
Have cenotaphed their patchwork with their names,
And on posterity enforced their claims,

XXXVII

On Trajan's column Saint Pietro preaches,
　　Where Trajan stood in days of Roman glory.
Saint Paolo (sword in hand) his doctrine teaches
　　Where Antoninus stood—so great in story !
And every year the wonder grows the larger
That Marc Aurelius sits upon his charger.

XXXVIII

That some ignoble Saint the noble brute
　　Has not bestrode, and sat in cope and mitre,
With a knight-templar standing at each foot
　　To keep him straight, and make him hold the tighter.
But saints unseemly look when placed astraddle
And soon grow sick when seated on a saddle.

XXXIX

Each tomb they plundered and each mausoleum,
　　Each temple of its marble works bereft,
Their urns and vases sent to their museum,
　　Their ashes to the winds cast right and left !
Unsepulchred the Cæsars from their coffins,
And lodged their own bones there 'mid scowls and
　　scoffin's.

XL

And every here and there you'll see large blocks,
  Of spacious tenements by walls enclosed,
Where monks and nuns in unproductive flocks
  Have long in sloth and idleness reposed.
Unprofitable drones, who ate the honey,
And sold their benisons for love or money.

XLI

Inhuman institutions, every hive !
  Where men and women in their youthful prime
Were taught to sacrifice themselves alive,
  And lead a life revolting in our time,
Sinning against the law given at man's birth
' Increase and multiply and fill the earth.'

XLII

And thus the city, like a human creature
  Defrauded of the food it lived upon,
Has preyed on its own vitals, lost each feature,
  And turned a skeleton of moss and stone.
Entailing ruin on th' entire nation
From the sheer want of healthy population !

XLIII

Acres where tens of thousands lived and died
  Are now large vineyards, or broad fields of maize,
Or wastes where thistles wave in prickly pride,
  Where goats and donkeys dearly love to graze,
Places where dust and rubbish may be shot,
Where cats and dogs may unmolested rot.

XLIV

And the Campagna, once a fruitful garden
    Filled with a happy and a prosp'rous people,
Where each Patrician had his country warden,
    And countless hamlets, showed both tower and steeple
Is now wild grazing ground for sheep and steers
A hunting prairie for cavaliers !

XLV

The very ground on which we tread is rich
    In human dust, as is a graveyard old.
Rare marbles one may find in ev'ry ditch,
    Whole capitals and columns in the mould.
The hills themselves have crumbled to decay
And filled the valleys with their fertile clay.

XLVI

Go to the Forum ! Mark its excavations
    Where scores of workmen daily sweat and toil,
Unearthing structures from their broad foundations
    Full thirty feet beneath the present soil.
The aggregation of two thousand years
By dusty Time, within this vale of tears.

XLVII

Go to the palace of the Cæsars.   There !
    Survey the wrecks of Vandals in their might,
From superjacent mounds of earth laid bare,
    By reverential hands now brought to light.
And wonder how humanity could ever
Such priceless works of art contrive to shiver.

Columns of granite, marble, alabaster,
   That might have stood unto the end of time,
Shattered to fragments as if made of plaster,
   Colossal statues of the true sublime,
Heads, arms, and legs, in endless mutilation !
Chipped into bits, with ruthless profanation !

Arches of brickwork, of stupendous span,
   More durable than rock itself, torn down !
Whilst shapeless turrets round the spacious plan
   On ruined altars, urns, and fountains frown,
On frescoed ceilings and mosaic floors,
And cenotaphs and epitaphs in scores !

On chips of Jupiter, Pan, Mars, and Juno,
   The Lares and Penates of old Troy,
On bits of Christian saints, Mark, Paul, or Bruno,
   And what destructive Time could not destroy.
On bricks and tiles, stamped with the very name
Of their own makers of transcendent fame.

The Goth and Hun, the Ostrogoth and Gaul,
   Were merciful to Roman fanes and Art,
These mounds of ruins that you so appal
   Were made by Christian Pontiffs ! Goths at heart !
Iconoclasts ! who 'gainst all idols raged,
And 'gainst all Pagan shrines destruction waged.

LII

Yet the late ruler of this ancient race,
  Claimed right divine to sway each faith and feature,
The gifts of prophet, priest, and king t' embrace
  In one poor perishable human creature,
Daring the world his dogmas to resent,
With threats of everlasting punishment !

LIII

And had himself INFALLIBLE declared,
  A demigod on Earth ! even GOD's VICEGERENT ?
By edict ecumenical prepared
  In the late inauspicious *sederunt*,
Which like Pandora's box, a host of evils
Let loose upon the world, like fiery devils.

LIV

What cant and casuistry we're doomed to bear !
  What family discords and what parish jars !
What rank intolerance, and hate laid bare !
  'Twixt sense and nonsense, what momentous wars !
'Twixt Church and State, what horrible confliction
To prove and to disprove the Pope's last fiction !

LV

Meanwhile stern Nemesis her Goths and Gauls
  Has launched against the pontifical throne ;
Already have they scaled Rome's sacred walls,
  And fierce defiance from their bugles blown.
Reason and common sense, and common weal
Now load the cannon and now point the steel.

LVI

The magic citadel now rent and riven,
  Is to its very deep foundation shaken,
And many a templar knight has died unshriven,
  And many a cross-key banner has been taken,
The garrison within oppressed with fears,
Of domes and turrets falling round their ears.

LVII

Another year has passed away, and fate
  Has brought us back within the walls of Rome,
Great are the changes in both Church and State,
  Italia here at last has found her home.
Here sit her senators and frame her laws,
Here dwells her king with bountiful applause.

LVIII

The pontiff's throne has crumbled into dust,
  The sceptre fallen from his enfeebled hand,
St. Peter's sword is crusted o'er with rust,
  And impotently waves his wizard wand.
The keys of heaven, which he professed to keep,
Mere lumbering symbols, to be purchased cheap.

LIX

The Roman people have outlived the sway
  Of pope and prelate, priest and monk, and nun ;
Rome's Church has fallen into extreme decay,
  The best of citizens its altars shun,
None but the very old and wretched there
Assemble at a sermon or a prayer.

LX

The Ecumenic Chamber's standing still.
  Gaudy in wainscot, painting, lathe, and plaster,
Where men, vain men, with dogmatising will,
  Tried common sense and reason to o'ermaster,
Until the world rebelled at their vast vanity,
And set its face against such dire profanity.

LXI

Confessors by the score, in every tongue
  Of modern times, sit there to hear confessions,
And grant indulgences to old and young,
  And absolution for each one's transgressions,
But rarely have we seen a single sinner
Accept the boon that made him such a winner.

LXII

The Vatican museum, long the glory
  Of modern Rome, and open unto all,
Where many a corridor, and many a story,
  And many a vaulted roof and marble hall
Sparkled with works of art, all rich and rare,
Can now be seldom seen—*by a backstair.*

LXIII

A special application must be made,
  Some days before the visit is intended,
Which when before the *major domo* laid,
  May be replied to, or may be contended,
Alloying thus with pain its greatest pleasure,
And souring the enjoyment of each treasure.

LXIV

Old Æsop tells us when the lion trembled
   In sickness and old age, and took to bed,
The more ignoble beasts around assembled,
   And kicked and worried him till he was dead ;
None more resentful than the silly ass,
Which took the lead as loudest of the class.

LXV

Thus sects of every phase of faith now gather
   From every quarter of the winds of heaven,
Around the sick bed of the Holy Father,
   By hopes of proselytizing hither driven,
And preach and pray against the Holy See
With fervent unction, and with license free.

LXVI

And heterodoxy with her hydra heads
   Has opened her pantheon in the city,
Each separate head a different doctrine spreads,
   Some transcendental and some only witty ;
But all opposed in tenets to each other,
Each Scripture-reader warring with his brother.

LXVII

No dogma now is safe, no papal bull
   Can show a horn without a fervent baiting ;
Each mythic relique, and each papal tool,
   Is torn to pieces with the fiercest rating.
Anathemas and excommunications
Are trodden under foot as profanations.

LXVIII

Indulgencies for sins, and benedictions,
  Are held so cheap as not to be worth asking,
And solemn texts are found out airy fictions,
  And modern credence greatly overtasking.
St. Peter's chains and bones pronounced all spurious,
And interesting only to the curious!

LXIX

The oldest dogma, that St. Peter filled
  The papal chair for five and twenty years,
Is now disputed, and divines well skilled
  In Scripture lore are dinning in our ears,
That Peter never set a foot in Rome,
And that a mighty sham must be his dome!

LXX

And face to face, like gladiators fierce,
  The champions of Dissent and of the Vatican,
Have held a tournament at point and tierce.
  St. Peter's sword 'gainst Methodistic yataghan,
And truth to tell the doctors of dissent,
Have claimed the day in that grand tournament.

LXXI

The chains that lately bound her Rome has cast
  Into a fiery furnace, sevenfold heated,
By popular resentful, hot-air blast,
  The clanking metal to the crown escheated
Is being welded into workmen's tools,
To reconstruct her city by new rules.

Old Porta Pia looks as well as new,
   The breaches in the walls built up securely,
A marble tablet tells the story true,
   That there Italian soldiers, acting purely
From patriotic motives, sealed the breach
And dared the Great Infallible to teach !

He who Rome's ancient walls expects to view
   Still standing, still defensive, will be foiled ;
A few foundation stones, a gate or two,
   On which skilled architects of old have toiled—
St. Peter's Mura Torta, and some tower,
Are nearly all the remnants of this hour.

The modern walls were built of brick and mortar,
   By new-elected popes, in poles and patches,
Who ticketed each section like a porter,
   With marble cenotaphs and long dispatches,
Their arms and names, tiara and cross-keys,
In hopes the thoughtless multitude to please.

And many a cornice from some heathen shrine,
   And lettered marble fragment figures there,
And many a head, once worshipped as divine,
   Is dovetailed 'mongst the bricks, at distance rare,
And marble stairs, and torsi all defaced,
Are used as kerb-stones in the reckless waste !

LXXVI

The pick and spade, the trowel and the hammer
  Are hard at work from morn to sunny eve,
All through the city runs continuous clamour,
  At every turn improvements you perceive ;
New roads, streets, squares, new palaces arise
Worthy of ancient Rome in style and size.

LXXVII

Herculean labours wait upon the State
  Throughout the length and breadth of the old city,
And Hercules himself is here, and great
  In muscle still, and cleansing without pity
The foul Augean stable, long the scorn
Of every sentient man of woman born.

LXXVIII

Those huge monastic piles of rude dead walls
  That filled the vacant eye at every corner,
With all their cloisters, cells, and banquet-halls,
  Are now no longer subjects for the scorner ;
New doors and windows, and new light of day
Have made them useful, to their monks dismay.

LXXIX

The troops of rope-girt mendicants of old,
  With shaven crowns, bare legs, and sandalled feet,
That jostled passers-by, in penance bold,
  And overcrowded every public street,
Have vanished from the scene, as have their betters,
Leaving amongst the populace no debtors.

M

LXXX

Their very bells, so often on the clang,
  Both day and night, regardless of all time,
Exciting many an oath, and many a pang,
  Are silent now, without one single chime ;
The world now goes to bed and sleeps in peace,
As if of life they had renewed their lease.

LXXXI

No mercenary bands in gay pelisse
  And mediæval toggery protect her,
But her own citizens preserve the peace,
  And make each foreign visitor respect her ;
Five thousand strong her city legions muster,
And do their duty gratis, without fluster.

LXXXII

Avaunt, ye fops, ye good-for-naught, ye ninnies,
  Who on the rich Forestieri forage,
Who mart your rank for dollars and for guineas,
  And sell your birthrights for a mess of porridge;
And lead a lap-dog life in splendid ease,
Your only duty day and night to please.

LXXXIII

The time draws nigh when healthy country-quarters
  Shall stud each Sabine and each Alban hill,
When armed patrols shall cease, and brigand Tartars
  Shall turn their hands to work with right good will ;
When Tivoli and Tusculum shall be repeopled,
And lonely Alba Longa be re-steepled.

LXXXIV

When oak and chestnut jungles must give place
  To smiling gardens and suburban features,
When hordes of swine that fatten there apace
  Shall be replaced by graceful human creatures,
And Rome a true Arcadia shall raise,
  Worthy an ancient Roman's fervent praise.

LXXXV

Bang goes a heavy gun from Hadrian's tomb,
  Shaking the windows of the papal palace,
All round Rome's seven hills runs the startling bomb,
  Shaking the young grapes on each reedy trellis,
No signal for assault or for alarm—
'Tis but the mid-day gun, and free from harm.

LXXXVI

Time was when true time was in Rome ignored,
  When church bells jangled forth each its own hour,
When ilka man's and woman's ears were bored,
  And ilka monast'ry proclaimed its power;
Now the true time is told to one and all,
And clocks and watches all obey the call.

CANTO EIGHTH.

I

Now whilst the British Isles are clothed in snow,
  And wintry weather is the daily lot,
And sea-coal fires on the hearthrugs glow,
  And rich plum-puddings simmer in each pot,
Let us our doors and windows open wide,
And welcome the warm sun with grateful pride.

II

The month of March is now but three days old
  Yet Spring has turned the corner of the year,
And bursting buds and blossoms manifold
  Delight all eyes, and makes the fields more dear;
The grassy sward embroidered o'er with flowers,
The atmosphere perfumed by rosy bowers.

III

Humblest but sweetest of the early Spring
  The violet and primrose now appear;
The bee and butterfly are on the wing,
  With crocus, jonquil, daisy, all so dear;
The almond and the plum-tree are in bloom,
And Winter has now found a grassy tomb.

IV

What mighty conflagration is in view?
  Sure Tivoli itself must be on fire,
Or some volcano broken out anew,
  Is burning up the mountains in its ire,
Flashing its flames along the Milky-way,
And putting out each star like light of day.

V

The Northern Hemisphere is in a glow;
  The very clouds appear as if to burn;
As if a dozen comets, hid below
  The dark horizon, flushed up each in turn.
The moonless vault is red with ardent light,
And ev'ry countenance appears more bright.

VI

Well, that's our friend Aurora Borealis
  Come rather far from home and from her station,
Sickened of everlasting-frozen châlets,
  In quest of sunshine and some recreation,
Like minor Northern Lights, as 'twere a duty
To dazzle all men's eyes with their rare beauty.

VII

But to be serious, we have seen with awe
  A mighty agent of Almighty power,
A spark, a flash of that electric law,
  Which from eternity until this hour,
Has kept our earth revolving round its pole,
And bound each sun and star in one grand whole.

VIII

You see that lubber skulking 'mongst the bushes
  With rusty gun at cock, prepared to fire,
He calls himself a sportsman ; doves and thrushes
  The largest game to which he can aspire;
One's fingers tingle to give him a shot,
And spoil his sport, and wing the heartless sot.

IX

Go to the market-place, and you may mark
  The sweetest song-birds strung up by the score,
The blackbird, robin, linnet, thrush and lark,
  Exposed for sale with pigs of the wild boar,
And what's enough to make a gourmand faint,
With porcupines, and hares, and does *enceinte*.

X

This is the hatching season of the year,
  When ev'ry bird's a father or a mother,
And ev'ry bird that's shot, it must be clear,
  Must leave some orphan'd family or other
To starve and die forgotten in the nest,
With maledictions boiling in each breast.

XI

For shame, Italia ! thus to allow
  Thy song-birds to be butchered for the spit ;
Go, make new game-laws, make a solemn vow
  That birds and beasts shall have protection fit,
To rear their young ones safe from poacher's gun,
And make it penal when the deed is done.

XII

Adieu, ye modern Romans and old Rome!
   Heaven aid your efforts for resuscitation;
An infant Hercules may you become
   The Strangler of the Pythons of thy nation,
And grow apace a Hercules in power,
Amidst the thunder-clouds that round thee lower.

XIII

Like old Laocoön, you struggled long
   Within the serpents' coils constricting round you ;
Thyself and sons, though stalwart men and strong,
   Writhing within the monster coils that bound you.
Now you have severed them with thy keen knife,
You'll prize the liberty of thy new life.

XIV

A great futurity is yet in store
   For long-sunk Italy and for her races !
Each man now hates the bonds he lately wore,
   And proudly puts his shoulder to the traces,
To draw the Car of State up from the mire,
And place it on the rail in fit attire.

XV

Now up the troubled Tiber's tawny tide,
   With snorting steed we wend our winding way,
Casting our wond'ring eyes both far and wide
   On green savannas and on ruins grey,
Mentana and Rotunda close at hand,
Where Garibaldi made his final stand.

XVI

There on the verge of liberating Rome,
  His Bersaglieri had to turn and flee,
Wat'ring with tears the unproductive loam,
  Cursing the French who dared them to be free,
And from each Roman forehead fiercely tore
The cap of liberty that Frenchmen wore.

XVII

There rebel Constantine, puffed up with pride,
  Maxentius fought, and conquered, and destroyed;
And plunging through the Tiber's bloody tide,
  Upon that flowery mead his force deployed,
And leading them unto Rome's city gate,
Of ancient paganism sealed the fate.

XVIII

The image of the cross upon the sky
  That led him on to victory and power,
He forthwith had displayed to ev'ry eye,
  And as his standard hoisted from that hour;
And Christianity embraced apace
As the religion of the Latin race.

XIX

Now up the channel of the foaming Nar,
  With panting engine sore oppressed we creep,
By many a broken arch and rocky scar,
  'Neath stately Narni built upon the steep,
Through boundless fields of barley, rye and wheat,
And endless villages all clean and neat.

XX

And now through old Etruria we steam,
  With grand old cities perched upon each hill,
By many a weeding band and oxen team,
  O'er many a viaduct and dribbling rill,
Where landscapes unsurpassed in rare fertility,
Contend in space with naked rock sterility.

XXI

Once more we tread a Carthaginian camp,
  The camp of Hannibal, first of his line,
O'er Spain and Gaul victorious, and the tramp,
  O'er snowy Alps and sunny Apennine,
Victorious still upon this fertile plain,
Loading its soil with tens of thousands slain.

XXII

There in the morning mist his bugles sounding,
  Brave Hannibal advanced into the thickets,
His buffaloes and elephants impounding,
  Crowning the heights and throwing wide his pickets.
Prepared to take the Romans by surprise,
Little expecting such a deep disguise.

XXIII

Swift marched the Roman army in pursuit,
  Picking up Punic trophies in each dell,
When down upon them rushed both horse and foot
  With sword and javelin, in one grand yell,
Clotting with gore the brambles of the brake,
And driving hecatombs into the lake.

XXIV

Red ran the Sanguinetto with their blood,
  Purpling the waters of the inland sea,
And Rome's best legions, broken in that wood,
  Before the Carthaginians dared to flee,
Leaving behind them tens of thousands slain
To whiten with their bones the blood-stained plain.

XXV

There ancient Rome's hereditary foes
  Were but a week's march from the city's gate,
With their vast heritage of hates and woes
  Boiling like lava under each breast-plate;
No wonder Romans trembled in their shoes
When of this battle they had heard the news.

XXVI

At last we stand upon the watershed
  Between the Tiber and the Tuscan Aar;
Strange conformation, ev'ry earthy bed
  Personifying rock and rocky scar,
Down which the rain-floods run in rapid chase
Washing the soil away adown each race.

XXVII

Unearthing the dry bones of beasts colossal
  That there had lived and died ere man was seen,
Iguanodons and mastodons all *fossal*,
  That browsed upon the palms and fern trees green.
When pterodactyles nestled in each brake,
And savage saurians harboured in each lake.

XXVIII

When herds of elephants, oppressed with heat,
  Shrank from the glare of a too fervent sun,
And sought in vain to find a cool retreat
  Before the evening twilight had begun.
Go to the rich museum in Firenze
And their acquaintance make in sober frenzy.

XXIX

Now down the Arno's crystal stream we run,
  With rapid pace, the engine at its ease,
By many a villa basking in the sun,
  And many a palace that a king might please.
With many a nightingale upon the spray,
And reached Firenze at the close of day.

XXX

Firenze, since we left your royal city,
  Great changes have occurred in King and Court,
And both have left you with a sort of pity,
  And in old Rome have fixed their chief resort.
But, nothing daunted, you have seen them part
Without a twinge of jealousy at heart.

XXXI

Let Rome remain the centre of the State,
  The fountain-head of liberty and law ;
Assemble round her all that's good and great,
  All that is worthy of the nation's awe !
Firenze can afford to live alone,
Without a parliament ! without a throne !

XXXII

Firenze can exclaim without a qualm,
   Avante, mia! with no niggard zeal,
And kiss her cheek, and lock her palm in palm,
   And work together for Italia's weal.
But Florence shall remain throughout all time
The choice resort of strangers of all clime.

XXXIII

Once more we mount the lofty Apennine,
   With tandem engines tugging at the train,
Stemming the mountains by a steep incline,
   And, looking down upon the Tuscan plain,
Behold the Arno in its overflow
Gleaming like gold beneath the sunset glow.

XXXIV

Soon as we gained the pent upon the chain
   Where nought but oaks and chestnuts seemed to grow,
One engine was returned unto the plain,
   The other the immense train took in tow,
And rattled down the Reno's rocky course,
The drag put on to curb its rapid force.

XXXV

A wondrous work of royal engineering!
   This mountain railway's made with signal skill ;
We hope its shares and dividends are cheering,
   And that its friends will keep it free from ill,
From falling rocks and beds of plastic clay,
And keep the passage clear both night and day.

XXXVI

Bologna ! cries the guard.   What strange sensation
   Now fills the platform with increasing roar,
The train is pulled to pieces in the station,
   One half goes on to Venice with its store ;
And now the very bulky Indian mail,
The Overland, is tacked unto our tail.

XXXVII

What loads of letter boxes it contains,
   From China, and Manilla, and Japan,
From Cochin-China, the Tycoon's domains,
   From Java, Singapore, and Hindostan,
From the Euphrates, Aden, and the Nile,
And many a Turkish port and Grecian isle.

XXXVIII

What extra loads of passengers there are,
   Young men on furlough with their sickly wives,
Old men distinguished for their deeds in war,
   Returning home to end their honoured lives ;
And widowed mothers with their babes unborn,
And even some spinsters with their hopes forlorn.

XXXIX

A lot of sallow children too were there,
   Saved from a lingering and a certain death,
With kidmutgars and ayahs passing fair,
   Some speaking Teligoo below their breath,
Some speaking Hindostani at full pitch,
In Oriental raiment every stitch.

XL.

Some Mandarins were there, some Japanese,
   Some Javanese, Malays, and even Australians,
Manillanese, and Mugs Shans, Cingalese,
   And Turks and Tartars, Arabs and Thessalians,
With many other Oriental races,
All keenly looking for their first-class places.

XLI

Italia has resumed her ancient sway
   And opened to the world her Port Brindisi ;
The commerce of the East there finds its way,
   The P. and O. have made the voyage easy ;
Their ev'ry ship is loaded to the gunnel,
With ready transit through the Alpine Tunnel.

XLII

Thou too art going home in grief,
   Widowed and sorrowful, in tears,
With no resource to give relief,
   With few kind friends to calm your fears,
A stranger in a foreign land,
Shipwrecked upon a fatal strand.

XLIII

When last we left you, hope was strong,
   That danger then had passed away,
And that his fellowship would long
   Through stormy life be thy mainstay.
Now he is gone !   Alas ! how sad !
And you are left in mourning clad !

XLIV

We cannot bid you not to weep,
　We dare not tell you not to mourn,
With loss so great and grief so deep,
　And heartstrings overstretched and torn,
The voice must falter, pulse beat slow,
The bosom heave, the tears must flow.

XLV

The hardest fate in life's to bear
　A faithful youthful consort lost,
The weeds of widowhood to wear,
　The mind by love and anguish tossed,
Even we most bitter tear-drops shed,
When hope was blasted, life had fled.

XLVI

Would we could give some antidote,
　Some potent magic-working charm,
To smooth thy brow and cheer thy lot,
　And place you out of reach of harm.
But Heaven alone can send such balm;
The tempest of thy sorrow calm.

XLVII

The rock from its foundation borne
　With shrubs and flowers is clothed anew;
The mountain-top by lightning torn,
　Becomes more beautiful to view;
The tree snapped off upon the plain
Fresh saplings soon sends forth again.

XLVIII

The castaway on desert isle
   Finds solace in expected sail ;
The mariners becalmed beguile
   Their time preparing for the gale ;
The ice-bound crew expectant wait
On summer, though it comes but late.

XLIX

Go ! seek relief in change of place,
   Of occupation, and of clime,
Serenity will come apace,
   And peace and cheerfulness with time.
The talents you possess employ,
You'll find in them a source of joy.

L

In prose and poetry engage ;
   Read History ! transfer ! translate !
Give every day's events a page,
   Foreign, domestic, or of State.
Let music occupy some hours,
And painting landscapes, fruits, and flowers.

LI

Devotion you will not forget,
   Nor alms nor charity neglect ;
Nor in vain cares and sorrows fret,
   Respecting all who you respect ;
Another consort you may find,
As warm in love, as good and kind !

LII

Parma and Mòdena, once so commanding,
    Long the abode of dukes of royal state,
With gorgeous palaces, both empty standing,
    Where are thy Estes and Farneses great?
Those Nepotes of Popes and Kaisers' cousins?
Gone to their last and long account by dozens.

LIII

Leaving their palaces and works of art
    Mortgaged unto the long-forbearing nation,
Fast running to decay in whole or part,
    Unless prevented by some liquidation.
A legacy no doubt somewhat expensive,
To keep in trim such tenements extensive!

LIV

Where are thy Guelphs and Ghibellines so fierce,
    Who fought like gladiators till they fell,
Ripping and running through in deadly tierce,
    Which Cinquecento history can tell?
Where are thy Scaligeri and Visconti,
And dozen other names, we could recount ye?

LV

Ask at their palace gates in every city;
    Their scutcheons will point out each old resort;
Their rooms of state let out, some out of pity,
    Most at low rental round each filthy court;
Ask at their cenotaphs, their tombs unurned,
And *fuimus* will be the tale returned.

N

LVI

All hail, majestic, ever brimful Po!
　Thy name must be engraved upon our heart,
For in our schoolboy days, how long ago
　It matters not, but then thou hadst a part,
And now we're glad thy image to renew,
And chisel it afresh, as is thy due.

LVII

Well we remember when thy tiny store
　Seemed but a step across unto the eye,
When even a mouse could jump from shore to shore,
　And even a flock of sheep could drink it dry;
Here thy abundance fills this boundless plain,
Its every water-way, and every drain.

LVIII

Ten thousand channels drain thy muddy tide,
　And waft its riches through ten thousand fields,
And spread fertility both far and wide,
　Where'er a husbandman his mattock wields;
Extending far to sea the fertile plains,
Nova Italia giving new domains.

LIX

Stupendous also is thy inundation,
　Flooding fair Lombardy just like a sea,
Driving its countrymen in consternation
　To seek for shelter on each roof and tree.
Yet, paying well for all their fright and toil,
With sundry inches thick of richest soil.

LX

Dottissima Pavia !   Long the seat
    Of Lombard kings, of law, and art, and science ;
Famous a thousand years ago !   Complete
    Thy university stands still in each appliance
To teach and train thy rising generation
To play their part on every state occasion.

LXI

Famous for thy most wonderful Certosa,
    Of matchless architecture every stone,
Each stone a work of art.   Quite *gloriosa !*
    Fit for a papal altar or a throne ;
Its frescoes, paintings, sculptures, carvings, gildings,
Found equalled only in most royal buildings.

LXII

A great atonement for a grievous crime !
    A grand sin-offering for a heinous sin !
Through which thy Galeazzo hoped to climb
    From hell to heaven, and an admittance win
By intercession of his patron saint,
Leaving behind him every bloody taint.

LXIII

And his salvation to make doubly sure,
    A sacred band of five-and-twenty monks,
In person and in faith all doubly pure,
    With well-stored larders and with well filled-trunks,
Were taught to pray for the Visconti line,
And preach it to an eminence divine.

LXIV

But even their prayers failed to save the shrine;
    Rapacious Frenchmen plundered the grand pile,
Cantoned their soldiers there like herds of swine,
    And turned the sacristy to uses vile;
Now only hands enough are kept in pay
To cleanse it and preserve it from decay.

LXV

Vice-regal city! prosperous Milano!
    Substantial in thy palaces and people,
Driving thy car of commerce so *piano*,
    And storing up thy wealth high as a steeple;
Though lake or river comes not near your city,
Yet your canals conduct to many a jetty.

LXVI

And pour clear streams of water through the town,
    And streams of merchandize from every quarter,
Thy butter, bacon, cheese, of old renown,
    Thy silks and salsiments for cash or barter,
Thy corn and wine, thy fruit and wool, thy treasure,
Thy citizens enriching beyond measure.

LXVII

Thy greatest glory is thy grand cathedral,
    Which all the world knows and all the stars;
The next is thy arcade, so octahedral,
    A Crystal Palace, or a *Champ de Mars*.
But sad to tell, our countrymen undoing,
For the big contract proved their utter ruin.

LXVIII

Around its octagon thy greatest men,'
    The greatest men of any age or nation,
Look down on their most humble servants, when
    They muster 'neath its dome, of every station,
To burn their weeds and spit on floors encaustic,
Even on its walls and arabesques fantastic.

LXIX

Large omnibuses, well equipped as any
    In Manchester or Paris, run in state,
And for the slender fare of but one penny
    From thy Duomo to each city gate,
Transport their charge in comfort and in ease,
Setting down all at any point they please.

LXX

No man is idle in the busy fray,
    Thy lazy monks and nuns, now few in number,
Are congregated in some central stay,
    And thy wide streets and squares no more encumber,
And their vast monast'ries, those vast abuses,
Are turned to public and to private uses.

LXXI

Thy city walls, a useless piece of lumber,
    You've tumbled down and gained a boulevard ;
The cost was great, and blastings beyond number
    Alone could bring them down—they were so hard—
Hard as the hardest of plum-pudding rock,
Which picks and iron crow-bars seemed to mock.

LXXII

Resurgam is your motto now. *Avante!*
    Each man and woman seems to take to heart.
Right through low hostelrie and shaky shanty,
    New open roadways run from part to part.
And yet the fine arts occupy thy care;
Thy Brera is replete with trophies rare.

LXXIII

A grand conception you have got on hand—
    A marble monument to Leonardo,
None grander will be found in any land:
    Da Vinci and his pupils *al riguardo.*
A city's pride, a people's admiration,
A contribution worthy of thy nation.

LXXIV

Now Lombardy's rich plains begin to rise,
    And gentle hills and dales to take their place:
The snowy Alps loom dim upon the skies;
    The clouds and mountains rivalling in grace,
More heavy lies the due of early morn,
More freshly blows the breeze upon the corn.

LXXV

'What boundless lake is that?' amazed you say,
    'No lake do I remember in these regions;
Yet there one stands but a few leagues away,
    Dappled with islands and lone trees in legions,
Reflecting like a mirror ev'ry tree
Upon its bosom in fine phantasy.'

LXXVI

No lake is there ! 'tis but the flickering haze,
   The morning moisture rising from the ground,
The rarely-seen *mirage*, which there displays
   The wondrous beauties which you thus astound ;
But evanescent as that silver cloud
Resting on the horizon like a shroud.

LXXVII

Now pass we Monza, famed for the Iron Crown,
   Theodelinda's, of most sacred story,
Presented by a Pope of great renown
   To Lombard's queen, enrobed in papal glory !
The rim wrought from a crucifixion nail,
And left unto her heirs by deed entail.

LXXVIII

Long worn by Austria's kaisers great in fame
   As the palladium of their Lombard realm,
Of late delivered o'er in fear and shame
   To Italy, now ruling at the helm.
Her king now wears it when it suits his pleasure,
Or locks it up as a most sacred treasure.

LXXIX

Let us descend from Camerlata's station,
   Adown the slopes to Como and its lake,
And bid adieu to railway swift rotation,
   And in the ' Volta ' an apartment take,
And pay obeisance to that man of mark,
Volta in marble ! Of the flashing spark !

LXXX

Nova Italia, grateful to her great men,
　　Is lavish of fine statues to each name,
To men of Art and Science, as to State men,
　　Putting our British Islands to the shame,
Where men are honoured by their butcher's bills,
Or by the margins of their dying wills.

LXXXI

Where men of Art and Science are ignored!
　　The greatest benefactors of our race,
Men whom old Greece and Rome would have adored,
　　Amongst the great bestatued find no place!
Even Jenner, though once made a man of mark,
Was hustled out of town and in the dark!

LXXXII

The statue of the man who saved his nation
　　From loathsome pestilence and dread mortality,
From frightful pock-pits and disfiguration,
　　Was not allowed to sit on an equality
With those whose greatest merit was to kill,
Or run the nation up the longest bill!

LXXXIII

' He's but a doctor!' is the canting cry,
　　And doctors go for nought when we are well;
But let disease step in, then ev'ry eye
　　Is fixed upon them like a very spell!
When late our Royal Prince was at death's door,
Whose footsteps were most welcome on the floor?

CANTO NINTH

I

LAGO DI COMO! dare we pen a verse
  On what a thousand pens have writ before?
And tried (perhaps, in vain) in metre terse,
  To vent their feelings, seated on thy shore,
As we are now, enamoured of the scene,
Screened from thy sunshine by thy laurels green.

II

A thousand skilful artists have pourtrayed
  A thousand tit-bits of thy land and water,
And the impartial world has not delayed
  To prize their paintings, sometimes no great matter;
Then why can't rhymesters write without a charge
Of saying nothing new, on cliff or barge?

III

Here Volta first drew breath, and lived, and died,
  Discovering his pile, and spark electric,
That took his name, and gave the world wide
  A messenger of light, a power eclectic,
That flits from isle to isle, from pole to pole,
As quick as thought arriving at its goal.

IV

These slender wires, now stretching overhead,
    Are but the railroads of his vital spark,
O'er which it travels from its plastic bed,
    In calm or storm, in daylight or in dark,
Distinctly telling 'mongst the kangaroos,
Our wants and wishes, and this morning's news.

V

That clerk now sitting by the light machinery
    Is talking with our cousins 'cross the Atlantic,
Or sending messages unto the deanery,
    Or chaffering in China for some antic;
And back the answers roll, fresh from the wheel,
In characters as clear and true as steel!

VI

Galvani! Volta! Franklin! What three men!
    With what successful efforts have they striven
To make discernible to human ken,
    The mysteries of life in earth and heaven!
Raising humanity unto the skies,
And dazzling with new light our wond'ring eyes.

VII

Let's step on board the steamer 'William Tell;'
    The steam is up, the bell upon the toll,
And make for Cadenabbia for a spell,
    And 'mongst its sprouting vines and fig-trees stroll;
Como within itself has few attractions,
Save some ecclesiastic, vulgar fractions.

VIII

The rising sun the night mist's slowly lifting,
    And rolling it in clouds up to the sky!
At every hundred yards the scene is shifting,
    New landscapes grand disclosing to the eye;
The Splugen under snowy blankets sleeping!
The nearer mountains in their nightcaps weeping!

IX

Their tears in streams, descending down their cheeks,
    From cliff to precipice, in white cascades,
Watering the cornfields in their mazy freaks,
    Or gurgling through some hamlet's grassy glades,
Or bursting from some rock in potent rill,
With power enough to turn a cotton-mill!

X

Clear is thy lake as is Castalian fountain,
    Many its fathoms deep and furlongs wide,
Bright châlets speck the slopes of every mountain,
    And one continued village is thy side!
With villas not a few aristocratic,
Mingling amongst their neighbours so erratic.

XI

The forenoon breeze is up, the upbound fleet
    Has slipped its moorings, hoisting every sail,
Right gallantly they carry loads of wheat,
    And casks of wine and oil, and fruit for sale;
The steamer dashes through them like a fish,
And lands us safe upon the strand we wish.

Few spots on earth are more divinely favoured,
   Than Cadenabbia seated on thy shore,
With tropical and temperate perfumes savoured;
   The more you know it you'll enjoy't the more,
Especially in autumn and in spring,
When tourists are most frequent on the wing.

The tide of travellers who take their chances
   In Sicily, or Naples, or in Rome,
And northwards steering as the spring advances,
   Led by the cuckoo and the swallow home,
Here find fit resting-place to plume their wings,
To grease their carriage-wheels, and cord their springs.

The vine is here the staple of the fields,
   Tied to a stake or on a trellis spread,
Right bountiful the loads of grapes it yields,
   The purple clusters ripening overhead,
Safe from the tourist or the village belle,
The only pilferer, gay Philomel!

To all strange uses do they train the vine;
   Sometimes to make a basket, or a fire,
At times for vinegar, at times for wine,
   At times to shade a pigstye, or a *byre*;
To ornament a cottage palisade,
Or cover in a palace colonnade!

XVI

The mulberry here grows its leaves in vain!
   Soon as to full development they spread,
They're torn from ev'ry twig with might and main,
   To feed the loathsome silkworms in some shed;
Creatures that spin their winding-sheet and die,
Or reappear next spring a butterfly!

XVII

Behold that butterfly upon the wing,
   Gilded and painted quite to admiration,
Sipping the honey of the early spring,
   And from each bluebell drawing a potation!
'Twas but a loathsome grub some months ago,
And now comes out just like a thing for show.

XVIII

A perilous position for the stranger!
   A goshawk marks it on the bending spray,
Regardless of exposure or of danger,
   And forthwith snaps it up as lawful prey,
And all triumphant wings his wicked way
In search of other victims all as gay.

XIX

And thus a human butterfly we've seen
   From her paternal domicile take wing,
Scorning old comrades of her village green,
   Snapping asunder every social string,
Voluptuous flaunting in expensive raiment,
Got by sweet promises of future payment.

XX

When some great woman-killer in his might
Encompassed her about, and fairly caught her,
And crushed the poor thing, trembling with delight,
Just as old Mother Eve's most erring daughter,
And wrested from her ev'rything she prized,
And left her, in his triumph, undisguised.

XXI

To praise the landscape seen from the Bellevue
Would tax the power of any mortal man.
If there's a paradise on earth, 'tis true
You'll find it there! So go and see't who can.
Enough for us its beauties to proclaim,
And certify its merits with our name!

XXII

Lugano! though thy Lago's more confined
Than Como's or than Maggiore's lake,
Yet lovers of the picturesque will find
Charms quite its own, which they cannot mistake,
Nestled amidst its mountains tipped with snow,
Or bordering its waters far below!

XXIII

Each Alpine peak, and precipice, and fell,
Each streak of morning mist and rosy sky,
Each hamlet, châlet, and each chestnut dell,
Can look down on its counterpart from high,
Marred only by the steamer's widening wave,
Or herd of cattle as their sides they lave.

XXIV

Although the streams that feed it are but few,
    And scanty in their tribute, one and all,
Yet every mountain-side, its mountain dew
    Pours down in torrents after a rainfall,
Making the lake at times to overflow,
And half the city inundate where low.

XXV

Here let us rest awhile, and take our ease
    In this most comfortable home—the Parc !
Where at this season folks are glad to squeeze,
    As our progenitors did in the ark ;
Only they enter and depart unknown,
Each day a new list having of its own.

XXVI

The Parc Hotel was once a hive of monks.
    In a rich garden looking on the sun,
With well-stored granaries and barns and bunks,
    A grand refectory and cells each one,
With a large church, all frescoed by a master
As great as any that e'er painted plaster.

XXVII

Swiss is the flag ! Italian is the people,
    A hybrid with the best points of each nation.
Right Catholic all ! as tell each tower and steeple,
    With their confounded bells, a great vexation !
The climate of that genial golden mean,
The mountain and the plain that lies between.

XXVIII

Terrace on terrace raised, the vineyards rise,
  The vines on elm and maple trees festooned
In wild profusion, and gigantic size,
  Whilst the poor husband trees are sternly pruned
Unto the stump, yea, almost unto death !
And left just twigs enough to save their breath.

XXIX

Thus, husbands, men of substance, we have seen
  Supporting wives extravagantly gay,
Drudging through life, subdued in mind and mien,
  Whilst their shrew spouses spent their hours in play;
Using their lords like elm and maple stumps,
Leaving them just enough to clothe their ———.

XXX

Thus ladies we have seen, with aches and pains,
 ' In fifty-guinea dresses, wondrous gay !
Sweeping the streets with their right royal trains,
  And ruining a silk dress once a day;
Whilst their sad husbands dressed in stable *tog*,
And lived on bread and cheese, or humbler *prog*.'

XXXI

And yet prolific mothers wonder why
  Men do not marry as they wont to do,
Why bachelors are now become so shy,
  And why young eligibles cease to woo;
They know full well the cost of modern wives,
And so live bachelors throughout their lives !

XXXII

Yet sickness, accidents, and death prevail
  Even in this favoured land and sunny clime,
And strangers not a few have had to wail
  Some comrade tourist, lost in manhood's prime,
And had to follow to their graves their biers,
And close their tours alone, in grief and tears !

XXXIII

Here whilst the pass is being cleared of snow
  By May-day sunshine, in unclouded splendour,
And opening buds and blossoms in full blow
  Delight the eye and make the heart more tender,
Let's rest awhile and dedicate a stanza,
Unto the scenery of proud Pallanza !

XXXIV

Its promontory stretching in the *Lago*,
  Clear as is crystal, spacious as a sea !
Where clouds and Alpine peaks throw their *imago*
  O'er perpendicular rock and myrtle tree,
Whilst oaks and mountains climb each mountain side,
And vineyards dip their tendrils in the tide.

XXXV

Now rhododendrons and magnolias bloom
  In rich luxuriance, the garden's pride !
The cactus, and the aloe, and the broom,
  With scores of shrubs and tropic plants beside,
Under a sky so genial and serene
One never can forget the *mise en-scène.*

o

XXXVI

Nor is the weather always halcyon here ;
  At times fierce squalls and heavy rains prevail
Striking the ferrymen with fervent fear,
  And driving into shelter every sail,
Rolling against the shore a lofty surf
And dappling with its foam the grassy turf.

XXXVII

The Borromean Islands charm the eye
  Like beauty-spots upon a comely face,
Each Isle a tiny realm, all high and dry,
  Without a reed or sedge around the place,
Where the shy nightingale its woodnote trills,
And even the dullest ear with music thrills.

XXXVIII

Here meet two Alpine roads from Schwytz descending
  Over the Simplon and St. Gothard passes,
Marvels of engineering, every bending,
  Forcing their way through cliffs and deep crevasses,
Up which or down, the postboys at a trot
From State to State career in action hot.

XXXIX

The snow-fed Tosa and Ticino pour
  Their foaming torrents down into the lake,
Whilst minor streamlets, numbered by the score,
  Into the rock-girt basin gently break,
And villages and villas everywhere
Along its margin stand in beauty rare.

XL

And rapid steamers rush from shore to shore,
    Chasing the finny shoals upon their course,
Whilst lazy cargo-boats with sail and oar,
    Transport raw merchandise with minor force,
Large paving-stones or loads of fertile loam,
Or granite masses for some church in Rome.

XLI

Those splendid columns which you so astounded,
    Within St. Paul's Basilica at Rome,
Were from that mountain torn and roughly rounded ;
    Were sent by raft and rail to their new home.
So very solid is the granite rock
We've four such columns seen wedged from one block

XLII

That man who spends a week upon this scene,
    'Mid springtide blossoms, or 'mid autumn fruits,
Has cause to thank his stars benign, we ween,
    And thank kind Providence for such pursuits.
In Mem'ry's waste such sunny spots will shine
Throughout his future life as things divine !

XLIII

Let this, the fifth of May, with due regard
    Be calendered in letters red as scarlet ;
That day we sleighed across the St. Gotthard,
    Hiding us from the cold like any varlet !
When warmest Mantas had no power to warm,
And for our freezing nose we felt alarm.

XLIV

Ascending from Airolo in slow motion,
  By endless zig-zags, cut into the schist,
At ten we reached the snow, just like an ocean,
  With wrappers manifold on limbs and chest;
And straight embarked each pair on board a sleigh,
A thing on skates just like a cabriolet.

XLV

Each sleigh by one big horse was pulled along,
  The motion like a boat's on a rough *See*;
With risk of being sea-sick, weak and strong,
  A train of thirty sleighs we ploughed our way;
So very silent slid each slippery team,
The transit seemed as if it were a dream!

XLVI

No bird of passage cleaved the mountain air,
  Not even a marmot showed his tiny head;
Nor tree, nor shrub maintained existence there,
  Each Alpine stream was frozen up and dead.
Feet deep in snow the kerb stones buried lay;
The telegraphic posts made known the way!

XLVII

Deep lay the snow for hours the pass upon,
  Smooth as the ocean swell on the Atlantic;
Cloudless the sky and brilliant shone the sun,
  But snell the north wind blew, and made us frantic.
Long icicles depended from each rock;
One's very vitals seemed to feel a shock!

XLVIII

At noon we reached the hospice on the top,
　And changing horses on the frosty pent,
We quickly skated down the northern slope,
　And gained the diligences upwards sent,
And rattled down to Andermatt to lunch,
Right well prepared to make a jolly munch.

XLIX

Now modern science and her engineers
　Have vowed to rob the pass of its *non volo;*
From Andermatt a tunnel it appears
　They've plann'd to drive right through unto Airolo.
With express railway trains both to and fro,
Right through the Alps, beneath their world of snow.

L.

Swift run we down the northern Alpine slopes,
　O'er dusty roads, the wheel upon the shoe,
Snell blows the breeze, nipping Spring's early hopes,
　And warning her to take no step to rue,
Whilst Winter on the uplands hovers near,
Prepared to make a foray in her rear.

LI

Her hardiest plants alone she trims with care,
　Like skirmishers wide scattered o'er the land,
The sloe, the plum, the almond, and the pear,
　Whilst all her tender plants she holds in hand.
Her birds, afraid of catching cold, are dumb!
Her bumble-bees have not begun to hum!

LII

Right busy is each peasant on his farm,
  Ploughing and digging ev'ry fertile plot,
Women and children lending all an arm
  (And empty stand each village and each cot),
Pruning their vines and training them in rows,
And rousing them from their prolonged repose.

LIII

Once more through Uri's Lake we skim the deep,
  With Rigi Scheideck still in winter slumber,
And Seelisberg high posted on the steep
  'Mid grand old pine-trees towering beyond number;
At last Lucerne, in the full blush of Spring,
Opens her doors to all upon the wing.

LIV

All hail, at last! united Father Rhine!
  Hail to thy deluge! Wonderfully grand!
Bursting upon the world, almost divine!
  The daily worship of this Vaterland!
With reverential eyes we gaze on thee,
Pure and transparent from thy Boden Sea.

LV

Familiar have we been with all thy sources,
  Amidst the Alps and everlasting snow,
And many a league we've wandered down their courses,
  Watching them mile by mile more potent grow,
By tens of thousand torrents rushing down
From ev'ry glacier, every mountain brown.

LVI

We've stood across thy Reuss, no trying task !
  A rough-shod foot implanted on each shore,
And poured libations from our spirit-flask,
  And reinforced its slender infant store.
Once more accept in thy stupendous might
A flask of *eau-de-vic*, in homage right!

LVII

Flow on, for ever flow ! thou wondrous river!
  In thy primeval magnitude at ease ;
Time on thy water lays no tax whatever,
  Nor dries thee up with age, nor with disease.
Thy river runs perennial in its flow,
The same now as a thousand years ago.

LVIII

In this lone corner of the wold
Five hundred years ago, as told,
Saint Uda built for us this fold
    Before life's sand had run.
The grandsires of these silver pines
That now o'erlook our ruined shrines,
Had they the power of making signs,
    Could tell what good was done.

LIX

Two hundred years are not yet sped
Since we our flocks to pasture led,
And fed them full on living bread,
    Within this sacred pile.

Saint Mary's altar gleamed in gold,
Frankincense rose in clouds untold,
And diapasons grandly rolled
    Throughout the vaulted aisle.

LX

Our abbots robed in rich attire,
Their nuns and monks led on in choir,
And one and all had their desire,
    Within each hallowed cell.
Each had his task like boys at school,
Waste not—want not, was our rule,
Despising every worldly fool,
    We ruralized right well.

LXI

We trimmed our garden, tilled our soil,
We grew our barley, flax and oil,
Our sturdy monks supplied the toil
    On *ora*-idle days.
We made our butter and our cheese,
Got wax and honey from our bees,
The best of wall-fruit from our trees,
    And corn-flour from our maize.

LXII

We grew our grapes and made our wine,
We brewed strong ale and reared fat kine,
The passing stream gave fishes fine,
    For holy fast-days' fare.

Our herd of sheep gave warm attire,
The forest kept us well in fire,
And ev'ry thing man could desire,
　　Was freely fostered there.

LXIII

Our neighbours kept us well in mind,
Paying their tithes when due in kind,
And none to our deserts were blind
　　In times of urgent need.
A plough or waggon was at hand,
A mettled steed at our command,
A mower, or a reaping band
　　Their word as good as deed.

LXIV

But Vandalism, fierce and fell,
Broke in upon us like a spell,
Unhinged each door, tore down each bell,
　　Unroofed our sacred dome;
St. Mary's image burned with fire,
And all our saints, in vengeance dire,
In fragments broke in frantic ire,
　　Like Goths and Huns in Rome.

LXV

Now sculptured columns strew the floor,
The living ivy wreaths each door,
The cenotaphs and tombs of yore,
　　Lie scattered small and great;

The ashes of our men of God,
Now fertilise the very sod
On which with naked feet they trod,
   In penitential state.

LXVI

Now cattle graze within our walls,`
The cuckoo from the turret calls,
And bats and owls enjoy the halls
   Where abbots wont to dine ;
And crowds of strangers come and stare,
And cry, Let all false saints beware ;
Destruction well her arm laid bare
   To wreck this Wicked Shrine !

LXVII

Here Baden-Baden holds her court
   And all the world obey,
Their *guldens*, the *beau-monde* to sport,
   The *demi-monde* to play.
Here London *roués*, Paris snobs,
And German Jews and Russian nobs,
And riflers sharp of foreign fobs,
   Delight to find their way.

LXVIII

Here's Jonathan in superfine,
   With ties as bright as May,
And daughters ultra-columbine,
   Superlatively gay.

Twanging queer English through their noses,
A Shibboleth that straight exposes
Their Yankeedom, and clear discloses
    Their grotesque love of *Liberté*.

LXIX

Here fortune-hunters hunt for wives,
    And Fortune's sons for pleasure,
Here mothers sell their daughter's lives
    To bears rich beyond measure !
Here gallants skilled in friendship's guise,
By falsehood and by coining lies
Escape confiding husbands' eyes,
    And rob them of life's treasure.

LXX

Here Harlotry unhives her swarms
    Of puffed and painted faces,
Parading their half-faded charms
    With meretricious graces.
Here prodigals their wild oats sow,
And rowdies rough more rowdy grow,
And modest ladies blush to show
    Themselves in such loose places.

LXXI

Here high-bred matrons may be seen
    With ungloved itching palm,
And high-bred damsels too, we ween,
    So keen, so fair, so calm!

Seated at table *tout le soir*
Staking their gold on *rouge et noir*,
Under some hoped-for lucky star,
　　Without a single qualm!

LXXII

Here blacklegs, knaves, and villains try
　　To ruin honest men!
Here sharpest wits with sharpers vie
　　To feather each vile den!
Here beggars on high horses ride,
And hell its portal opens wide,
And hellish fiends all hellward slide
　　Never to rise again.

LXXIII

Here invalids both high and low
　　Resort to bathe, and drink
The lukewarm waters as they flow,
　　And o'er their sins to think.
Yet water fit to drink is rare,
The water of the Oos we dare
To say smells like a cesspool, where
　　The city drainings stink.

LXXIV

Conservancy's neglected here!
　　The principles of health
Nor thought of, nor protected here,
　　With all its ducal wealth,

They've but one stream in all the town,
And it is dyed a whitey brown,
A *cloaca!* of no renown
　　Beyond offensive filth.

LXXV

A hot place Baden is at best
　　With little ventilation !
Shut in by hills, north, east, and west,
　　Its atmosphere's stagnation.
Where strangers spend so much a year,
They have good right to better cheer:
A sound untainted atmosphere,
　　Pure water for potation.

CANTO TENTH

I

BEHOLD the stern realities of war,
   Its pomp and panoply now passed away !
Where rubbish, wreck, and desolation mar
   The splendid landscape and the brilliant day;
Where Kehl in smoky ruins mourns alone,
Prosperity and population gone.

II

Let's leave behind us Kehl and ruins dire,
   Its blood-stained walls and putrifying moats,—
The first to bear the brunt of Gallic fire,—
   And cross the Rhine upon the bridge of boats,
And take a bird's-eye view of fair Alsace
From the cathedral tower with opera glass.

III

The very trees are ruined where they stood,
   Some with a round shot sticking in the timber,
Some splintered, shattered, sawed across, as good,
   To mend some baggage-cart, or broken limber.
The very solid ground on which we tread,
Is charged with broken shells and solid lead.

IV

The homesteads of the living broken down,
    The homesteads of the dead were there invaded;
That graveyard was a post of high renown,
    Its marble slabs and tombstones greatly aided
The sieging operations, and its soil
Gave ready sepulture in the turmoil.

V

A shell exploded in that vault profound,
    And blew it open to the winds of heaven;
Some dozens pitted there the open ground,
    And by a bolt of iron that wall was riven;
And many a battered tomb still bears the mark
Of leaden bullets fired in the dark.

VI

What heterogeneous mass of men is here!
    Smothered in clouds of dust, footsore and lame!
Driven on like cattle, guarded front and rear!
    Bending beneath the burden of their shame!
Rueful and sad, like malefactors led!
Unarmed, ill clad, apparently ill fed!

VII

French prisoners of war, released in truth,
    By German soldiers driven home to France!
Part of the Strasburg garrison in sooth!
    About to enter Strasburg in advance,
Which they defended gallantly and well,
As records of the war will no doubt tell.

VIII

Let us approach the outworks, and survey
  The sieging operations, marshes, ditches,
Already mantled o'er with new-grown hay,
  With melons, pumpkins, cucumbers, and vetches,
Where thrifty matrons tend a cow or two,
Or spread their linen on the evening dew.

IX

These rudely heaved-up ramparts, now so green,
  With notches cut into them, black and brown,
Were German batteries, for Krupps, we ween,
  Whence shot and shell were launched into the town.
The odour of the guns is smelt there still,
And cartridge-tatters dapple every hill.

X

What ruthless circumstance of war was there!
  What sad destruction! what hair-breadth escapes!
The very bombs conflicting in the air!
  The splinters showering down in thousand shapes;
Easier it was a hail-storm to escape
Than these fell showers of shrapnell and of grape.

XI

A hundred yards apart, or may be more,   [graves.
  There stood the guns! There stand the gunner's
Some tenanted by one, some by a score.
  At midnight hours entombed, in wide camp caves;
Short was the service, silent sank the dead,
Not even a rush-light lighted them to bed.

XII

Green grows the grass upon each humble mound,
  All marked with crosses, lettered with a knife ;
With sea-pinks not a few are bordered round ;
  Some bear a garland from some weeping wife ;
A few are cenotaphed with costly art ;
A quick-set hedge protects the burial part.

XIII

Let us approach the breach beyond these ridges,
  Up which the German legions rushed amain,
And *vorwarts* cross the ditches and the bridges,
  And the parade and boulevard attain.
The gate's with German soldiers now defended,
Some under arms, some on the ground extended.

XIV

Mark well that avenue of bricks and mortar ;
  Through that the storming party led the way !
The road into the city made the shorter,
  O'er ruined houses in the last affray.
The prefecture's a shell of blackened walls ;
And see that statue, which the sight appals.

XV

A prefect with a grape-shot through his head,
  Two through his legs, still standing on his feet ;
With all this mortal dose of solid lead,
  Maintaining his composure all complete !
The shot-holed walls around him as quiescent,
As a fair face from small-pox convalescent.

P

XVI

There the cathedral stands, a glorious pile!
 Of old red sandstone, sculptured to satiety,
With grotesque figures, wondrous in their style:
 Saints, sinners, seraphims, in strange variety,
The spire a perfect gem of filigree,
As medieval knight could wish to see!

XVII

Let us ascend the tower, and look around
 Upon the pent roofs of the antique city.
There shot and shell marks are but rarely found,
 As if the gunners' hearts were moved by pity.
Not sixty shots in all we think you'll find,
On the cathedral walls, of every kind!

XVIII

Each piece of patchwork new upon the roofs
 Denotes a shot-hole from a German gun;
And sooth to say, they furnish ample proofs
 That cannonading was discreetly done,
Much less destruction was effected far
Than is the use and wont of ruthless war!

XIX

The greatest loss was in the Bibliothèque,
 Burnt to the ground with all its books and shelves,
A world of literature, sad to reflect,
 Lost to posterity and to ourselves.
The gallery of paintings also fell
A prey unto the flames, to shot and shell.

XX

We looked for Frenchmen, but we looked in vain,
  The citizens seemed German to a man,
All eager in pursuit of honest gain,
  Their language German, and their journals ran
In German letters, and each sign and street
Figured in German characters complete.

XXI

French soldiers there were there, sad and dismayed,
  From Switzerland and Germany returned,
In party-coloured uniforms arrayed,
  Courting the courtesy they lately spurned;
But public peace and plenty seemed secured,
Each man and woman in their rights ensured.

XXII

Now on through fair Alsace we rail along,
  O'er boundless plains all green with waving corn,
Each field a battlefield, where right and wrong
  Fought for supremacy, with deadly scorn,
Where Germany and France put forth their strength
In most gigantic armies, miles in length.

XXIII

Now the scene changes; picturesque Lorraine
  With hills, and dales, and streams, delights the eye,
The *beau idéal* of a duke's domain !
  Where all that's rich and rare in beauty vie;
Where even the earth below with wealth abounds,
Its caverns rich as are its open grounds.

XXIV

Grand-ducal Nancy, once the seat of power!
  Of fortune, honour, letters, beauty, art,
Thy very weakness in thy evil hour,
  Was thy protection, when three Uhlans smart,
Rode right into thy city single-handed,
And off thy magistrates thy keys demanded.

XXV

A German general now rules in state,
  Where ducal potentates long ruled of yore,
And German sentinels now guard the gate,
  And German officers lodge on each floor
Of thy grand-ducal palace; German bands
Protect thy denizens from roguish hands.

XXVI

Yet truth to say they do their warding mildly;
  The bugle or the drum is seldom heard.
No swaggerers are seen patrolling wildly,
  But all conduct themselves with due regard.
Vae victis! is ignored in word and deed,
None daring to molest the bruised reed.

XXVII

Now *we* have entered Metz and stand entranced
  Upon its ramparts, gazing o'er the plain,
Where the French armies lately camped and pranced
  Under their general-in-chief, Bazaine;
All round the city walls his hosts were pitched,
Securely posted, hedged around, and ditched.

XXVIII

Crowning the heights a league or more away
  There stand the forts, the bulwarks of the camps,
Protecting all within them as they lay
  Ingloriously at ease, like idle scamps;
Whilst far beyond and out of sight there stood
The German cordon in most patient mood.

XXIX

Cutting off all supplies by night or day,
  Resolved to make them starve and then surrender,
Repulsing all attempts to steal away,
  Compelling them at last their arms to tender
As prisoners of war, and cross the Rhine
In shame and anguish, like a herd of swine !

XXX

Where Frenchmen lately mounted guard and strutted
  With all the fussiness of little men,
Broad-shouldered German sentinels are hutted,
  Speaking a jargon quite beyond our ken.
Bavarians, Saxons, Prussians, Polonese,
Munching big sausages and lumps of cheese.

XXXI

Where Famine, War, and pestilence late reigned,
  Health, Peace and Plenty reign in power supreme ;
Where cats and dogs and rats and mice were trained
  To grace the table, in their want extreme,
Now beef, and pork, and mutton take their places,
Worthy of highest praise and longest graces.

XXXII

Where muddy water late was best of cheer,
  Drawn from the ditch, the Sielle, or the Moselle,
They slake their thirst with cyder, wine, and beer,
  And of French hardships painful stories tell,
When even dead horseflesh was esteemed good meat,
And donkey steaks were bought at rates discreet.

XXXIII

How strange that Metz, the bulwark of the land,
  Should be a prison for its best defenders!
Should be a man-trap on a scale so grand,
  And change its heroes into mere pretenders.
The ever-restless, ever-meddling Gauls
Here learned a lesson that all France appals.

XXXIV

But one short year ago we passed through France,
  Amidst prosperity on ev'ry hand,
And saw its warlike demon at a glance
  Possess the populace throughout the land;
The thirst for glory burning in each breast,
Which nought but victory could set at rest.

XXXV

Vain, volatile, and proud of martial fame,
  Once more France threw her gauntlet o'er the Rhine,
And her hereditary foes, whom none could blame,
  Picked up the challenge o'er their cups of wine,
And took the field with unabated breath,
And fought it out even to the very death.

XXXVI

Now German garrisons in every town,
  Upholding public order may be seen;
The citizens with sense of shame borne down,
  And dragging servile loads from morn to e'en,
Cursing their stars which led them on the way,
Cursing themselves for being led astray.

XXXVII

Stern in their retribution, her late foes
  Material guarantees now hold in hand;
Great victories were not enough for those
  Who rolled invasion back from Fatherland;
The cost of war, even to the utmost thaler,
France now must pay to those who thus enthrall her.

XXXVIII

But France had greater shame than this to bear;
  Her foes were merciful compared to friends;
Look into Paris, count the ruins there,
  Her palaces burnt down by Frenchmen's hands,
By Red Republicans, those demons dire,
To glut their vengeance and accursed ire.

XXXIX

Blush, Paris, that such demons you could rear!
  That men and women too should thus combine,
Unawed by future punishment and fear,
  To wreck thy capital so wondrous fine.
The Germans spared each palace, dome, and steeple;
The wreck you see was made by thine own people.

XL.

An air of grief pervades each loyal face ;
    A look of pain and shame thy humblest orders,
Thy higher classes have decamped apace,
    Deserting house and home for the sea borders,
Half-peopled and half-ruined, gaunt and vague,
Poor Paris seems reviving from the plague.

XLI

A sad requital for a people's sin !
    Stern Nemesis her fasces there unbound,
And stripping France unto the very skin,
    Scourged her until she fell upon the ground,
Charging her to remember through all time,
That rapine was a nation's greatest crime.

XLII

Now for a Parthian shot at all hotels,
    Swiss, German, or Italian, everywhere,
Against them all our appetite rebels,
    Though there be some exceptions here and there,
Their keepers think we English come abroad
Merely to starve and die upon the road.

XLIII

Their dog's-meat messes and their cat's-meat fids
    Of what in earnest they call beef and mutton,
Their vegetables, only fit for kids,
    Would turn the stomach of a very glutton,
Their fish which never saw a living river,
Pike, perch, or tench, and salmon rarely ever.

XLIV

Their tea and coffee are a crying shame,
   Their cream, mere milk and water, whitey blue,
Their butter anything you like to name,
   Their bread oft sour, and always much too new,
Their eggs half-filled, half-stale, ofttimes inedible,
A state of things you must not think incredible.

XLV

Their fruit, though fruit in plenty's to be got,
   And good too, if one's careful in selection,
Is but the rubbish of each market lot,
   Half-ripe, half-rotten, not worth the dissection;
And then their puddings, cakes, and tarts are made
By numbskulls, knowing nothing of their trade.

XLVI

Their wines look superfine upon the *carte*,
   And by their prices any griff would think them.
But taste them, and their *gout* will make you start,
   And swear at any price you will not drink them:
Five francs a bottle is too much to pay
For stuff that's only fit to throw away.

XLVII

Their cooks—the villains! *chefs* indeed yclept,
   Ought to be forced to drink their own *potage*,
Ought with a cat's-tail to be soundly whipped,
   And sent to bed to sup on their own *rage*.
We came abroad our clothes a tight fit on us,
Now like a prodigal's they hang upon us.

XLVIII

Sharp practice is the golden rule of all,
    Their fittest sign-post is ' The Golden Fleece;'
Smaller and smaller grows each portion small,
    Yet year by year their charges all increase.
We lately ate two breakfasts at a sitting,
Served by mistake, and of the fact unwitting.

XLIX

Once more old England's chalky downs arise,
    Late hidden by the restless, heaving sea, .
And Dover Castle, towering to the skies,
    And Shakespeare's Cliff far off upon our lee,
With Deal and Margate smoking on the shore,
And heavy iron-clads moored upon the Nore.

L

Deep in that bay, beyond the Sheppey Island,
    Britannia's ships are built and sent afloat;
You see their tall masts looming o'er the dry land,
    Part of the Albion's crew now man that boat;
Her captain, proudly seated in the stern,
Asks for a passage up as you discern.

LI

And see, like two twin liners chained together,
    The Great Leviathan appears in state,
Safe back from laying the Atlantic tether,
    That Jonathan and John brings *tête-à-tête*.
Now they discuss each others *pro's and con's*
As in a chamber, like two doughty dons.

LII

Far as the eye can reach, craft without number
  Are seaward sailing down the ebbing tide ;
Parts of their cargo still their decks encumber,
  Whilst inward-bound ones at their anchors ride,
Rusty and weather-worn, with flags apeak,
Their numbers at the truck in bunting meek.

LIII

And that's an Indiaman, now outward bound,
  With all her crew and passengers on board,
And cheerly goes the capstan round and round,
  Right well her coops with fowls and ducks are stored,
The long-boat filled with sheep, fit for the knife,
And sties of pigs, all doomed to a short life.

LIV

Her stern festooned with hampers, bags, and baskets,
  Filled with the very best of oilman's stores,
Made fast by ropeyarns, and by used-up gaskets,
  Pumpkins, and cabbages, and yams in scores ;
And a milch cow and calf are stowed away
Under these bulky bales of last year's hay.

LV

The passengers assembled on the poop
  Look joyous all, and pleased with future prospects,
As if it were against the law to stoop
  To sad misgivings or to blasted cross-specks ;
Young brides, bright spinsters, majors and cadets,
Fill up the captain's list,—right good assets.

LVI

Yes ! that's our dear old ship, the ' Nadir Shah,'
   In which whilome we sailed to sunny Ind,
When hope was strong and health without a flaw,
   And nothing came amiss, or calm, or wind.
Full many a storm we've both rode out since then,
Yet both are to the fore, though old stout men !

LVII

And where are the compatriots of our youth ?
   The gallant ships and still more gallant men
Who seemed built for a lengthened life in truth,
   All hale and strong as we ? Not one in ten—
One in a hundred only—now survives,
All ending one by one their shortened lives.

LVIII

Some ships went down in a Chinese typhoon.
   Some sprang a leak and sank in smoothest sea,
Some stranded at Madras in the monsoon,
   Some were abandoned on most urgent plea,
Some to their own destruction were decoyed,
Some by an open enemy destroyed.

LIX

A few were scuttled by their mutineers,
   A few were burnt in port at anchor riding,
A few were wrecked amidst their hopes and fears,
   A few were lost at sea without a tiding.
The dry rot and teredo spoiled a few,
A few were cast away by their own crew.

LX

The Nadir Shah, the Akhbar, and Mysore,
  Of Honourable John's once potent fleet,
Are but the few survivors to the fore,
  Sea-worthy still with all their gear complete.
That wondrous fleet that made Britannia great,
Ruling the seas in oriental state.

LXI

As for our fellow-men, more wayward still
  Was the stern destiny reserved for all :
Some fell sad victims to their own self will,
  Some perished in a midnight city brawl,
Some broke their skulls in sorely tempting Fate,
Some broke their necks in leaping o'er a gate.

LXII

A host lie buried on Australian shores,
  A host were massacred by Akhbar Khan,
The Jumna and the Ganges drowned some scores,
  Some hundreds fighting fell in Hindostan.
Many were slaughtered by the mutineers,
By men they led to glory of late years.

LXIII

Sunstroke and fever. cholera, the chase,
  The jungle and the camp in alternation,
Had each its victims in the rapid race
  Of tropical existence and prostration.
Some died by their own guns, by their own spears,
Some fell in duels, fighting with their peers.

LXIV

'The insolence of office, and the spurns
   That patient merit off th' unworthy bore,'
Off martinets and nepotists by turns,
   Gifted with power and patronage in store,
Made many a right good fellow wince and smart,
Blasted his prospects, and even broke his heart.

LXV

Some in dismay succumbed to doubts and fears,
   Some lost their senses and were invalided,
Some died by their own hands in blood and tears,
   Some from the Honourable Lists were weeded,
Some of the boldest of the youthful band
Died at their posts by the assassin's hand.

LXVI

The Honourable John himself is dead !
   Himself the victim of assassination.
Her Majesty the Queen reigns in his stead;
   The Company expired in degradation.
That Company which ruled with royal sway,
Which lords and dukes were willing to obey !

LXVII

The founder of an empire which extends
   Wide as both France and Germany together ;
The best of masters and the best of friends,
   Its servants ' loved it like a very brither ; '
Its subjects, Hindoo, Mussulman, and Seikh,
Revered its government, though strong yet meek.

LXVIII

Green grow the grass upon its humble grave !
  Sweet bloom the blossoms ! gently blow the wind !
Let palm leaves ever o'er its ashes wave !
  We ne'er shall see its like again in Ind !
'Stabbed to the heart by London rivals fell,'
Is all the epitaph its tomb need tell !

LXIX

Our stately steamer stems the rapid stream,
  The custom-house official jumps on board,
And we are roused as from a pleasing dream
  By 'Sir, your keys are wanted by my lord ;'
And though some passengers looked quite appalled
Our luggage was discreetly overhauled.

LXX

Now Woolwich we have reached. The tide is turning;
  Most ships are swinging round upon their chains,
And lo ! one run ashore is wildly burning,
  But little 'bove the water now remains.
A Spaniard ! with a crew of lazy dogs,
Laden with sugar and mahog'ny logs.

LXXI

That's Shooter's Hill now looking on the tide, [tered,
  Where Sir John Falstaff filled his paunch and blus-
And Mrs. Quickly wagged her tongue and sighed,
  And merry Hal the fat knight sorely flustered,
And Bardolph, Nym, and Pistol filled their gizzards,
And cursed and lied just like so many wizards.

LXXII

That's Greenwich and its palace at the landing,
  Once tenanted by England's worn-out tars;
Now tenantless, deserted, empty standing!
  Where no old sailor now can bless his stars.
Yet fit withal to house a noble king,
Or in the centre or in either wing.

LXXIII

And that's an Indian transport you admire,
  One of a lot of others of its class,
Fit to transport a regiment entire,
  With light and heavy baggage at a pass,
Right through to Hindostan by the Canal—
The Suez—to Bombay or to Bengal.

LXXIV

That ugly looking monster of huge power,
  With mighty cannon peering through its ports,
And mightier still, revolving in its tower,
  Manned by a Turkish crew of many sorts,
Was lately launched the Sultan's fleet to grace
And help him to assert his pride of place.

LXXV

And there, far inland 'yont the Isle of Dogs,
  The India Docks both East and West extend,
Mid sedgy marshes and deep miry bogs,
  Where nought but frogs and toads can claim a friend;
Yet there the commerce of the world is stored,
And everything but commerce is ignored.

LXXVI

And now we cross the Tunnel at full power,
  Where runs a railway train, both night and day,
From Middlesex to Surrey every hour,
  Beneath the muddy Thámes's waterway;
The archway waterproof! well lit and dry!
With all the comfort of the open sky.

LXXVII

Now the plot thickens, and the spacious river
  Is crammed with ships of every naval nation.
Hopeless the task of landing there, if ever;
  A snail's pace is our speed on *this* occasion.
And there a coal-barge, loaded to the water,
Is swamped and sunk, as if a daily matter.

LXXVIII

And now at last the ship has ceased to roar,
  And anchored in the stream with scores of others;
We wonder how the deuce to get on shore,
  Which more than any hitch the landsman bothers;
So all at once, to cut the matter short,
We hailed a waterman, of the right sort,

LXXIX

To row us to a penny boat hard by,
  And offered him a shilling for the job;
The fellow scowled at us contemptuously,
  As if his family we meant to rob.
Not less than two-and-sixpence would he take,
Although we felt disposed his head to break.

Q

LXXX

Once more afloat, aboard the ' Waterspinster,'
    Another voyage we must yet perform,
One penny for the passage to Westminster,
    Insured against high seas, lee shores, and storm,
Awed by the domo of our British Wren,
Amidst vast multitudes of busy men.

LXXXI

Straining in competition for dear life !
    Losing or winning, daily, nightly, ever !
Some hopeless bankrupts in the dreadful strife !
    Some millionaires, by sea, or land, or river !
Trampling their way upon the heaps of slain,
In hot pursuit of nothing else but gain.

LXXXII

The means of transit here are quite astounding,
    The bridges groaning 'neath oppressive drays,
The passengers on foot are so abounding,
    That all too narrow are the broadest ways ;
And trucks and cabs in every alley battle,
And railway trains along their bridges rattle.

LXXXIII

The bridges graceful, picturesque and grand,
    Of granite or of iron, in size stupendous,
The city's pride ! the wonder of the land !
    Arching safe roadways o'er a tide tremendous,
All as immovable as are the rocks
From which were blasted their enormous blocks.

LXXXIV

And steamers by the hundred ev'ry hour
  Flit up and down, with human creatures freighted,
Of wood or iron, high pressure or low power,
  All overcrowded, greatly overweighted,
Landing a score or two at every station,
And picking others up in due rotation.

LXXXV

The very sea seems rushing into dry land,
  As if it meant the country side to drown ;
And many a garden plot and spit of high land
  Is deluged by the spring-tide in the town ;
And lumbering barges inwards waft their cargo,
Like straws upon the stream without embargo.

LXXXVI

Behold the Thames' Embankment, stretching far
  As eye can reach along the crowded strand,
Without an archway or a break to mar
  Its granite architecture.   Simply grand !
Worthy the World-City's pomp and pride !
Worthy to curb the fury of its tide !

LXXXVII

Well we remember when the beach was crammed
  With filthy barges filled with filthy lading,
When the foreshore with slush and mud was dammed,
  And transit got through every nuisance wading,
And cats and dogs, and rats, and rags, and bones,
Usurped the space enclosed by these fine stones.

LXXXVIII

Well we remember that full thirty years
  Were spent in agitation of the scheme,—
The pros and cons, the wishes and the fears
  · That the vast project would turn out a dream,
How vile conflicting interests opposed it,
And its projectors cautiously disclosed it.

LXXXIX

Now a grand thoroughfare into the City
  Along the spacious masonry extends,
A railway through it, and full many a ditty
  Is sung amidst its gardens by its friends;
And soon we hope to see a splendid street
Stretch all along it, of construction meet.

XC

Now with the floating iron-built wharf we close,
  Westminster Stairs with right good will we climb;
Its minster, glorious pile! still perfect, shows
  Its antique turrets of the true sublime,
Marred only by St. Meg! there out of place!
A useless adjunct! void of size or grace!

XCI

No nobler gothic pile in our wide round,
  Than its New Palace have we ever seen;
No houses so august! none so profound!
  In legislative wisdom, none so keen!
Yet strange to say, the knotty Ballot Bill,
The bill of last year, is their subject still!

XCII

Most mighty city, London! much abused
  By thine own millions, far beyond endurance,
We left you hid in smoke and soot, and mused
  How you could best initiate a curance;
We now return, and find you hid in stink,
Just like a cuttle-fish in its own ink.

XCIII

This is the eighth of June, the day infernal,
  The elements themselves appear at war,
Quite equinoctial, and all life external
  Forbidding under pain of a catarrh;
The chilly air, a gelid sort of bath
Of smoke, and soot, and sleet, with miry path.

XCIV

Thy very atmosphere with smoke is tainted
  We blow the nuisance from our stuffed-up noses,
Thy ev'ry denizen with soot is painted,
  And on a bed begrimed with smoke reposes;
Go, spend a part of thy enormous wealth
On thine own grates, for sake of public health.

XCV

Science is ready with effective plans,
  To burn thy nuisance and effect a saving
To thy coal burners and their chimney cans,
  All doubts and dreads and difficulties braving.
Consult her! pay her with no stinting, mean,
And trust to her to make great London clean.

XCVI

Let us descend into the Underground—
   The Metropolitan—and rail our way,
And make the subterranean circuit round,
   Unto Tyburnia, our quondam stay;
Like moles through tunnels 'neath the noisy town,
'Neath streets and squares, and greens, and hillocks
      brown.

XCVII

Another masterpiece of engineering,
   Worthy of London and its monstrous trade !
The streets above too circumscribed appearing,
   The earth below their feet is useful made,
Through which its millions rush from point to point,
All in right order, nothing out of joint.

XCVIII

Now up the lofty flight of steps we mount,
   And reach the open air and light of day,
And hail a cab, and all our luggage count,
   And try the transit o'er the Queen's highway.
Zounds ! What a torture o'er big broken stones !
Enough to lame the horse and break our bones !

XCIX

What strange abuse of liberty and law !
   What fell contractors dare to mend our roads
With stones big as one's fist, and yearly draw
   Their handsome rates for their accursed loads?
We'd like to pay them off at twenty paces
With their own stones for all their vile disgraces.

C

Why have we not got tramways through the town,
    The greatest boon unto a busy city?
Most continental towns have laid them down,
    Even slow Vienna, which we view with pity.
London is ready with her plans and pay,
But parliament, perverse, obstructs the way.

CI

Our tours and retours now come to an end,
    Our continental circuit is completed.
No broken arms or legs have we to mend;
    Not ruined, though a good deal, no doubt, cheated;
A flea-bite the worst injury endured,
But property and person both secured.

LONDON : PRINTED BY
SPOTTISWOODE AND CO., NEW-STREET SQUARE
AND PARLIAMENT STREET

www.ingramcontent.com/pod-product-compliance
Lightning Source LLC
Chambersburg PA
CBHW030733280326
41926CB00086B/1301